SUMMER SMARTS

Activities and Skills to Prepare Students for 5th Grade

Jeanne Crane Castafero and Janet van Roden

Houghton Mifflin Company
New Ways to Know℠

Dear Parents,

What is the purpose of *Summer Smarts*?
Summer Smarts is a summer workbook that enables your child to review knowledge and reinforce skills learned in fourth grade. The intent of *Summer Smarts* is not to teach but to provide a bridge between fourth and fifth grades.

How does *Summer Smarts* differ from other workbooks?
Summer Smarts contains a unique integration of material, combining the traditional grade school subject matter into one workbook. *Summer Smarts* is a concise, direct way for your child to review the grade she or he has just completed. The instructions are to the point. Although the materials are fun and often surprising, it always is sensible material with a point.

How should *Summer Smarts* be used?
The worksheets in *Summer Smarts* are arranged in logical sequence, moving from easier concepts to harder ones. In order to take advantage of the sequencing and integration, we suggest that the workbook be done in order.

The reading books are an integral part of *Summer Smarts*. Although the worksheets for the reading books are found at the end of *Summer Smarts*, we encourage your child to space the reading books throughout the summer and not save them until the end.

What sort of reading books are used in *Summer Smarts*?
A lot of care has been taken in choosing the books used in our reading section. Since pre-fifth graders vary greatly in their reading ability and interests, we have also provided a section where your child may choose his or her own book. If the books we have chosen are not the right reading level for or not of interest to your child, use the free selections to adjust the level of difficulty.

Please keep in mind the obvious: children are incredibly different! We do not want your child to dread *Summer Smarts*. Use discretion about the pace at which you use this workbook and even about how much of the workbook your child completes.

There is an answer key located at the end of this book to assist you and your child.

Have a great—and smart—summer!

Sincerely,

Jeanne   *Janet*

Jeanne Crane Castafero and Janet van Roden

Contents

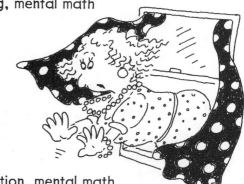

World History and Geography

2 Who Are you?   Reading comprehension, context clues, general knowledge

6 Where Do You Live?   Map work, general knowledge

9 You and Your World   Writing

10 Is This Greek to You?   Place value, money, rounding, mental math

12 Food Fungus   Science

14 A World of Knowledge   General knowledge

16 Remainders on Mount McKinley   Division

17 Feudalism   Reading comprehension, fact-opinion

19 A World of Analogies   Analogies

20 World Class Math   Decimals, time, division, multiplication, mental math

22 Passage to America   Topic sentence, supporting details, transition, conclusion

24 Mountains High   Graphing

26 Where in the World?   Geography

Sports and Leisure

28 Ancient Olympic Games   Reading comprehension, vocabulary

31 Baseball Riddle   Math computation

32 Olympic Geometry   Geometry terms, polygons

35 Modern Olympic Games   Reading comprehension, vocabulary, writing

38 High-Flying Fractions   Mixed and improper fractions

39 Making Music   Reading comprehension, math

42 Exercise Your Mind   Solid figures

43 Marble Math   Equivalent fractions and simplest form

44 Music to My Ears   Science, making instruments

46 Factor Trees   Factoring, decimals

Weather

48 Our Changing Weather Reading comprehension

51 A Drop of Fractions Working with fractions

52 Windy Poetry Verb tense, reading comprehension, parts of speech

54 Put on Your Poet's Hat Writing poetry

56 Weather Math Time, median, range, mean, place value, rounding

59 How's the Weather Reading a weather map

61 Weather You Like It or Not Perimeter, area, volume

63 Great Whirling Winds Punctuation

64 A Storm of Math Comparing and ordering fractions, decimals

65 Predicting Weather Changes Making a barometer

67 Weather News Using the newspaper, the 5 Ws, poetry writing

69 A Downpour of Division Division

70 Tornadoes Adjectives and adverbs, reading comprehension, math

72 Flip, Turn, and Slide Congruent figures

BOOK SECTION

74 *The Fighting Ground,* by Avi

77 *A View from the Cherry Tree,* by Willo Davis Roberts

79 *On My Honor,* by Marion Dane Bauer

82 Poet's Corner Free reading choice

85 Summarizing Free reading choice

87 Wow, That Was Some Story! Free reading choice

89 Answer Key

WORLD HISTORY AND GEOGRAPHY

Who Are You?

Humans have lived on Earth about 2,000,000 years. However, it was not until about 5500 years ago that they began to write and record history. How much do you know about the history of humans? Follow humankind's development as you work through a short history of the world. Fill in the blanks using the words in the boxes at the beginning of each section.

Pharaoh
artifacts
Julius Caesar
Cro-Magnon Man
Mesopotamia
pyramids
Neolithic Period
Zeus

This goes pretty fast, so fasten your seat belt to visit the earliest humans!

The first human is thought to have lived on Earth about two million years ago. The name of the earliest human most like us was **(1)** _____.

We have learned about him from archaeologists who study bones, cave drawings, and man-made objects called **(2)** _____. Examples of artifacts are pottery and tools.

The first humans were hunter-gatherers. Eventually, around 10,000 B.C., in a period known as the **(3)** _____, humans developed their knowledge of farming.

Now that we have put prehistoric man in a nutshell, let's see what we can do with the ancient world.

Somewhere around 3000 B.C., the first cities grew up in a fertile area known as "The Land Between Two Rivers." This land between the Tigris and Euphrates Rivers on the continent of Asia was called **(4)** _____. At first, Mesopotamia was ruled by the Sumerians, who built cities filled with narrow streets and houses made of mud bricks.

From 3100 to 31 B.C., Egypt developed as a great civilization on the banks of the Nile River. The Egyptian king was called

(5) _____. The Egyptians used slaves to build temples, tombs, and statues of their gods and goddesses. Today in Egypt you can still visit the great tombs built for kings, called

(6) _____.

Egypt was not the only great civilization in the ancient world. During this period, other civilizations developed in what is now known as the Middle East, China, and India.

Around 900 B.C., Greek civilization began. Religion played an important part in Greek life. The king of the Greek gods was

(7) _____.

Although many ancient civilizations became powerful, the empire of Rome was the largest and last of the ancient world. Rome eventually conquered all the lands around the Mediterranean Sea and all of western Europe. Perhaps the most famous general and dictator of the Roman Empire was

(8) _____. The Romans built roads, formed armies, and spread their language, laws, and customs throughout their empire.

How was that for flying through time? Look out Middle Ages! Here we come!

The Roman Empire became so large that it was difficult to rule. Invasions from many outsiders weakened it and eventually the Roman Empire became less powerful. The age after the decline of the ancient Roman Empire is sometimes called the (9) _____. It is an age that is often depicted with knights and castles.

William Shakespeare
Charlemagne
Middle Ages
Aztecs and Incas
Muslims
Declaration of Independence
Columbus, da Gama, and Magellan
Crusades
Louisiana Purchase

The most important leader during the Middle Ages was

(10) _____, known as "Charles the Great."

He conquered most of western Europe and united it under a great Empire.

Charlemagne was crowned king of the Holy Roman Empire by the pope.

Christianity thrived under his rule. In time, this Christian empire clashed

with the Arab followers of the religion of Islam who were called

(11) _____. From about the year 1100, and

continuing for almost two hundred years, religious wars known as the

(12) _____ were fought.

Good-bye Middle Ages! Hello Age of Exploration!

The 1400s were the "Age of the Exploration," when

such men as (13) _____

traveled the seas to find new lands. The most famous

English playwright (14) _____

was writing his plays just around the time the first English

colony of Jamestown was settled in America.

The first residents of North and South America were

not the explorers. Indian civilizations such as the

(15) _____ had formed

quite advanced societies in South America, while Indian tribes such as

the Shawnee, Iroquois, Cheyenne, and Pueblo thrived in North America.

When the European settlers came to America, they changed the Indians'

way of life forever. The Indians were forced to share their land with the

settlers. The English colonies in North America declared their independence from

England in 1776 by signing the (16) _____.

In 1803, the United States doubled it size with the purchase of land

from France called the (17) _____.

CHRONICAL

Civil War

Alan Shepard

Henry Ford

Martin Luther King, Jr.

Orville Wright

World Wars

Industrial Revolution

Sally Ride

Sandra Day O'Connor

Americans began to move West in covered wagons. Around 1848, thousands of people moved to California when gold was discovered there.

Now that we have the settlers in America, we are going to abandon the rest of world history and look at modern American history.

Around 1850, life changed drastically in America. New inventions enabled machines to manufacture things previously made by craftspeople. Factories and new industries changed people's lives. This revolution was known as the **(18)** _____ and marked the beginning of modern America.

Let's fly from here.

Beginning in 1861, America fought a war over slavery called the **(19)** _____, or the War Between the States. By 1903, **(20)** _____ flew the first successful airplane. In 1913, **(21)** _____ invented the assembly line for producing automobiles. In 1920, women in America were given the right to vote. The United States fought two **(22)** _____ beginning in 1914 and then again in 1941. In the 1950s and 1960s, the Civil Rights Movement led by **(23)** _____ fought to gain equality for blacks in America.

In 1961, **(24)** _____ was the first U.S. astronaut in space. In 1981, **(25)** _____ was the first woman on the Supreme Court. **(26)** _____, in 1983, was the first American woman in space.

Whew, did we ever race through that! The history of the world in just four pages! This is just a "mini" history of the world. What happened throughout the world last year alone would fill volumes of books!

180°
160°
140°
120°
100°
80°
60°
40°
20°
0°
20°
40°
60°
80°
100°
120°
140°
160°
180°

80°
60°
40°
20°
0°
20°
40°
60°
80°

6

WHERE DO YOU LIVE?

Use the map of the world on the previous page.

1. On the map, label north, south, east, and west in the appropriate boxes outside the outline of the world.

2. Lightly color in the continents as follows:

   South America = yellow   North America = green   Australia = red

   Asia = purple   Africa = orange   Europe = brown

   Antarctica = blue

FACTS
The lines that run east to west around the earth are called lines of **latitude**. The equator is 0° (zero degrees) latitude. Everything above the equator is called north latitude. North latitudes go from 0° at the equator to 90° at the North Pole. Below the equator are the south latitudes from 0° at the equator to 90° at the South Pole. On the map, latitude numbers are printed along the sides.

3. On the map, find the equator and color it black.

4. On the map, trace the north and south latitude lines in red.
   Then, circle the latitude degree numbers on the side in orange.

FACTS
The lines that run from the North Pole to the South Pole are called lines of **longitude**. Longitude lines are also measured in degrees. The longitude line running through Greenwich, England, is known as 0° longitude, or the Prime Meridian. Everything located to the right (east) of Greenwich on the map has an eastern longitude, and everything located to the left (west) has a western longitude. On the map, longitude numbers are printed on the top and bottom, and they go from 0° to 180°

5. On the map, trace the east and west longitude lines in green.
   Then, circle the longitude degree numbers on the top and bottom in purple.

Latitude and longitude lines are used by map makers to divide the world into sections. This way, every place in the world can be pinpointed by naming the latitude and longitude (called coordinates) closest to where a place is located.

6. Find the "X" on the continent of Australia.

   What is the approximate latitude? _____ degrees south

   What is the approximate longitude? _____ degrees east

7. Locate where you live on the map and draw a star.
   What is its approximate latitude and longitude? Answer
   with both degrees and direction.

   _____

8. Name 2 continents located in the longitudes west of the Prime Meridian.

   _____   _____

9. What country is located at each of the following coordinates?

   a. 30°N, 90°E _____

   b. 60°N, 120°W _____

The world is full of so many wonderful things! Many people find great pleasure in traveling to see both the natural wonders and the man-made treasures of the world. Match these natural wonders and treasures to their location.

_____ Grand Canyon	**a.** Moscow, Russia
_____ Big Ben	**b.** Paris, France
_____ Red Square	**c.** Agra, India
_____ Wailing Wall	**d.** China
_____ Taj Mahal	**e.** Pisa, Italy
_____ The Great Wall	**f.** London, England
_____ Eiffel Tower	**g.** Jerusalem, Israel
_____ Leaning Tower of Pisa	**h.** Western United States
_____ Pyramids	**i.** Egypt

You and Your World

How will you fit into this fast-moving world of ours? What would you like to do with your life? What would you like to be? Write a topic sentence and at least three complete sentences about what you would like to contribute to this world.

Topic Sentence: _____

_____

Supporting Details (3): _____

_____

_____

_____

_____

_____

Draw a picture of you as an adult.

Is This Greek to You?

1. Write these numbers in standard form.

   a. ninety-six million, five hundred six _____

   b. 74 million, 2 thousand, 12 _____

   c. 9,000,000, + 400,000 + 2200 + 1 _____

2. Write these numbers in word form.

   a. 7,426,005 _____

   b. 1,000,020 _____

3. What is the value of the 5 in each number?

   a. 6,549,212 _____

   b. 7,453,330 _____

   c. 807,459 _____

4. Round to the

   a. nearest thousand   6,822 _____

   b. nearest hundred   739,424 _____

   c. nearest thousand   99,900 _____

5. What would be your change?

   a. Cash given is $50.00

   Cost is $29.72   Change: $_____

   b. Cash given is $175.00

   Cost is $149.89   Change: $_____

6. **a.** Make $0.25 using 4 coins. _____

   b. Make $0.10 using 6 coins. _____

   c. Make $0.40 using 5 coins. _____

7. Circle the greater of the two money amounts. Then, write the coins or bills you would need to add to the lower number to make the two amounts equal. Use the smallest possible number of coins and bills.

   a. $2.98 $5.00

   _____

   b. $10.00 $5.88

   _____

8. Order these numbers from least to greatest.

   a. 652,640   752,800   719,820   _____

   b. 320,300   346,879   324,400   _____

9. What is the elapsed time between

   a. 10:00 A.M. and 3:50 P.M. _____

   b. 12:00 P.M. and 10:30 A.M. _____

10. Solve these problems in your head.

   a. 960 − 110 = _____   c. 260 + 310 = _____

   b. 680 − 230 = _____   d. 450 + 150 = _____

11. Solve these problems with pencil and paper.

   a. $33.98 − $7.69 = _____

   b. 4500 − 491 =   _____

   c. 5001 − 483 =   _____

12. Last year your school sold 2456 pencils with its logo. This year it only sold 1994.

   How many more pencils were sold last year? _____

Food Fungus

For much of history, the technology to refrigerate or preserve food did not exist. Food spoiled easily. One thing that spoils food is a form of fungus called mold. Mold spores are all around us—in the air, on our furniture, on our clothes, in our beds, and on our skin and hair. Mold grows and reproduces very quickly, especially in warm, moist, dark places.

Following is an experiment to help us learn about mold.

Materials

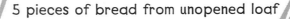

5 pieces of bread from unopened loaf

5 sealable plastic bags

5 labels

a toaster and refrigerator

Instructions

1. Remove one piece of bread from the loaf and touch it all over. Put it in a sealable plastic bag, seal it, and label it "Handled."

2. Remove a second piece of bread and handle it in the same manner. Put it in a bag with a few drops of water. Seal it and label it "Handled/ Moisture."

3. Remove a third piece of bread. Again handle it and put it in a bag and seal it. Label it "Handled/ Refrigerated."

4. Wash your hands thoroughly with soap and hot water. Carefully remove a fourth piece of bread, touching it as little as possible. Put it in a bag and seal it. Label this bag "Not Handled/ Not Toasted."

5. Remove a fifth piece of bread. Touch it as little as possible. Put the slice in a toaster and toast it. Remove it without much handling. Put it in a bag and seal it. Label "Not Handled/ Toasted."

6. Put the bag marked "Handled/ Refrigerated" into your refrigerator. Put the other bags in a dark cabinet. Make a note on the calendar to check the bags in two weeks.

7. After two weeks, gather the bags and answer questions 1–6.

1. Which breads grew the most mold? Rank the breads from most to least moldy and list them below.

   Most Moldy _____

   2nd Most Moldy _____

   3rd Most Moldy _____

   4th Moldy_____

   Least Moldy_____

2. Is mold more likely to grow when food is handled or not handled?

   Why do you think that is true?_____

3. Is mold more likely to grow when food is toasted or not toasted? _____

   Why do you think that is true?_____

4. Is mold more likely to grow when food is kept chilled or when it is stored

   at room temperature? _____

   Why do you think that is true?_____

   _____

5. Is mold more likely to grow when there is moisture or when food is dry? _____

   _____

   _____

   Why do you think that is true?_____

6. Based upon the conclusions you have drawn about which factors make food more likely to grow mold, what suggestions do you have for people who prepare and serve food?

   _____

   _____

   _____

   _____

   _____

A World of Knowledge

Write the correct answer in the column on the right.

1. What does the contraction **can't** stand for? _____

2. What letters do people write on an invitation when they want you to respond? _____

3. Who wrote the Declaration of Independence: George Washington or Thomas Jefferson? _____

4. Name the smallest continent. _____

5. How many times is the moon full each month? _____

6. Name the world's tallest mountain. _____

7. What ocean separates North America and Asia? _____

8. Is Denver in Maine or Colorado? _____

9. Which is bigger, church or a cathedral? _____

10. In what country are the Great Lakes located? _____

11. How long does it take Earth to rotate on its axis? _____

12. Is France in Europe or Asia? _____

13. How is Dan's mother's brother's daughter related to him? _____

14. Who is on a $1 bill? _____

15. Are the pyramids in Egypt or England? _____

16. Is a snake warm-blooded or cold-blooded? _____

17. Is Australia in the Northern or Southern Hemisphere? _____

18. Which continent has the most people, Africa, Asia, or Europe? _____

19. What Roman numeral comes before X? _____

20. How many inches is a half a foot? _____

21. Who has more money, a peasant or a lord? _____

22. Where is our federal government located? _____

23. Which is drier, a desert or an oasis? _____

24. Which happened first, the Crusades or the American Revolution? _____

25. Is Asia in the Eastern or Western Hemisphere? _____

26. With what is a moat filled? _____

27. What is a year with an extra day called? _____

28. Who supposedly sewed the first American flag? _____

Circle the word that does not belong.

1. apples	peas	peaches	pears	oranges
2. lip	nose	eye	hand	ear
3. catcher	outfielder	shortstop	pitcher	quarterback
4. volleyball	figure skating	basketball	football	baseball
5. California	Washington	Colorado	Detroit	Oregon
6. rattler	lizard	python	cobra	boa

Remainders on Mount McKinley

Math problems that involve remainders make you think! When you have a remainder, you must determine what it means in each case. As you work the following problems, think about how to use your remainder.

1. One hundred twelve people are going to tour Mount McKinley, the highest mountain in North America. Each bus takes 15 people. How many buses will be needed to take the tourists to the mountain?

   _____

2. The first group of 15 tourists collects 356 small rock samples. If they divide up the rocks equally and give the extras to the **youngest** member in the group, how many will the youngest member in the group get?

   _____

3. It takes 25 tourists to fill an entire page in the sign-in book at the base of Mount McKinley. If they start at the top of a new page, how many pages will the 112 tourists fill **completely**?

   _____

4. Mount McKinley is 20,320 feet high. Mount Everest, the highest mountain in the world, is 29,028 feet high. How much higher is Mount Everest than Mount McKinley?

   _____

5. The tourists each get a souvenir key chain upon completion of their trip. The key chains come in boxes of a dozen. How many boxes are needed in order to give each tourist a key chain?

   _____

16

FEUDALISM

During the Middle Ages in Europe, warfare was a way of life. The peasants, who were the villagers and farmers, were in need of protection from invading armies. They turned to the rich and powerful lords and noblemen who had the money and men to protect them. A system known as **feudalism** developed.

Under the feudal system, each state was ruled by a **king or prince**. He owned all of the land but gave large areas of it to his nobles in return for their loyalty. Many times the nobles would show their loyalty to the king or prince by gathering armies to fight for him.

The nobles would divide up their large estates into smaller units called **manors**. They would give these manors to **knights** in return for their loyalty and their pledge to fight for the noble and for the noble's king.

On every manor there were large groups of peasants called **serfs** who worked the land. To reward the serfs for working his land, the knight would promise to protect the serf and his family. The serfs were very much like slaves. All of the serfs, including women and children, had to work. They did the everyday work of the manor, such as working in the fields, milking cows, shearing sheep, making clothing, and building shelters. They could not leave the manor without their lord's permission.

Many nobles lived in big stone or wooden castles on the manor atop steep hills or in the midst of deep moats. The serfs would live outside the castle walls. In the event of danger, they and their livestock would find shelter within the castle walls. The manor would include many buildings other than the lord's castle. The manor might have a priest's house, a church, animal sheds, a blacksmith's shed, a mill to grind grain into flour, and a brewery to make beer. The manor would include many one-room huts with dirt floors and no windows for the serfs. In addition, the manor would include woods, farmland, and pastures. In all, the manor could be a thousand acres and was a self-contained town.

Circle the correct answer or fill in the blank.

1. While not directly stated, it can be reasoned that _____.

   a. the lords of the manor were all cruel men

   b. there was no good reason for feudalism to exist during the Middle Ages

   c. feudalism did not operate on the principle that "All men are created equal"

2. This article as a whole is about _____.

   a. describing a manor during the Middle Ages

   b. a way of life during the Middle Ages called feudalism

   c. comparing serfs to slaves

3. Feudalism developed in large part because peasants needed protection.

   a. yes   b. no   c. does not say

4. Which word in the second paragraph means "faithfulness"?

   _____

5. Which order reflects the classes in a feudal society?

   a. prince, nobles, knights, serfs

   b. nobles, prince, knights, serfs

   c. prince, nobles, serfs, knights

6. Label each statement fact or opinion.

   During feudalism, the manor was much like a town or village._____

   During the Middle Ages, all of the serfs had a very sad life. _____

Read About It To read more about knights and castles, try a funny short chapter book called *Knights of the Kitchen Table*. It's by Jon Scieszka with illustrations by Lane Smith, the talent behind *The Stinky Cheeseman* and *Math Curse*.

A WORLD OF ANALOGIES

An analogy shows a relationship between two pairs of words. A shorthand way of expressing this relationship is an analogy.

- **Here are a sentence and an analogy that compare words that mean about the same thing (that is, they are synonyms).**

Sentence: *Rules* are similar to *laws*, just as colleges are *similar* to *universities*.

Analogy: *Rules* are to *laws* as *colleges* are to *universities*.

- We can compare two words that are opposites, too (that is, they are antonyms).

Sentence: A *victory* is the opposite of a *defeat*, just as a *win* is the opposite of a *loss*.

Analogy: *Victory* is to *defeat* as *win* is to *loss*.

- An analogy can also show that one word names a part of another thing.

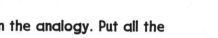

street	famous
play	computer
coastal	the National League
dry	south

Sentence: A *country* is part of a *continent*, just as a *planet* is part of a *solar system*.

Analogy: *Country* is to *continent* as *planet* is to *solar system*.

Decide the relationship of the first two words in the analogy. Put all the words in a sentence to help you figure out the relationship. Then, choose a word from the word box to finish these analogies.

1. *Thin* is to *skinny* as *well-known* is to _____.

2. *Chapter* is to *book* as *act* is to _____.

3. *Ocean* is to *sea* as *road* is to _____.

4. *Tall* is to *short* as *wet* is to _____.

5. *Mountain* is to *valley* as *north* is to _____.

6. *Drought* is to *flood* as *landlocked* is to _____.

7. *Hand* is to *body* as *keyboard* is to _____.

8. *Chicago White Sox* is to the *American League* as *Chicago Cubs* is to

_____.

WORLD CLASS MATH

1. Write the missing digit or digits in each problem.

```
   6 9 2 4           2 ☐ min   4 ☐ s          1 0 ft   8 in
 + 2 1 7 ☐         − 3 min     ☐ 2 s        − 9 ft   6 in
   9 0 9 7           3 min    2 6 s            ☐ ft    ☐ in
```

2. What is the value of the 9 in each number?

   a. 3.09 _____

   b. 224.9 _____

   c. 21,335,459 _____

3. Circle the equivalent decimals in each line.

   a. 6.7   6.07   6.70

   b. 10.40   10.45   10.4

4. Write these numbers in word form.

   a. 869.53 _____

   b. 9.871 _____

5. Write these numbers in decimal form.

   a. twelve and three thousandths _____

   b. six hundred thousand forty-two and seventy-three hundredths _____

6. At the last dance, 77 students bought tickets at $1.45 each.

   How much did the students pay in all? _____

7. If a spider could spin 675 yards of web a day, how many yards

   of web could it spin in a week? _____

8. Write the product for each problem.

```
   1.42        157.30
 ×   6        ×    2        3.41 × 4 = _____
```

9. Fill in the missing time.

   a. 9:20,   9:35,   _____,   10:05

   b. 3:00,   3:15,   3:30,   3:45,   _____,   4:15

10. If you can do five word problems in 15 minutes,

    how many can you do in one hour? _____

11. Multiply.

    a. $6 \times 942 =$ _____

    b. $7 \times 5083 =$ _____

12. Divide.

    a. $524 \div 7 =$ _____

    b. $395 \div 4 =$ _____

13. Do these problems in your head.

    a. $5 - \frac{3}{4} =$ _____

    b. $80 \div 20 =$ _____

    c. $90 \times 30 =$ _____

14. Two numbers added together are 13. Their product

    is 42. What are the numbers? _____ and _____

15. $100 \times$ _____ $= 10,000$

    $10 \times$ _____ $= 100,000$

16. What is Obi's favorite football team? _____

    Obi like the Eagles better than the Falcons.

    Obi like the Redskins better than the Steelers.

    Obi like the Steelers better than the Eagles.

Passage to America

A paragraph is made up of a group of sentences about one topic.
A good paragraph must

- state the topic of the paragraph clearly
- give supporting details
- order the details logically using good transition
- have a solid concluding sentence

Sample Paragraph

For the twelve million immigrants who passed through Ellis Island hoping for a better life in America, the trip must have been very stressful. First, for many immigrants, getting to the port to board the boat was their first trip away from home. Second, many immigrants left behind mothers, fathers, sisters, brothers, aunts, uncles, and friends. Third, for the immigrants, most of whom were trapped in the lower decks of the ship, the trip to America was often a nightmare. Conditions were dark, crowded, and unsanitary. Finally, upon their arrival in America, many immigrants found themselves in an unfamiliar land, unable to speak the language, and without friends. However, many immigrants have said that their arrival in Ellis Island was the greatest moment in their lives.

1. The topic sentence in the paragraph states the main idea. What is the main idea of this paragraph?

   _____

   _____

2. This paragraph's topic sentence is supported by four main details. Those details "prove" the topic sentence. Briefly restate those details.

   a. _____

   b. _____

   c. _____

   d. _____

3. The details are held together by "transition" words or phrases. The transitional words used in the paragraph above are **first, second, third,** and **finally.** Find the transition words and circle them.

4. A concluding sentence sums up the paragraph and reminds us of the topic. In your own words, what does the author conclude?

_____

_____

Now it is time for you to write a paragraph. Here is your topic:

There is a connection between history and geography. The food that people eat, the clothes that they wear, and the work that they do are influenced by the surroundings. Using (a) a topic sentence, (b) at least three supporting details using good transition, and (c) a concluding sentence, write a paragraph that explains why many early civilizations chose to settle along bodies of water such as oceans, rivers, and lakes.

_____

_____

_____

_____

_____

_____

_____

_____

_____

_____

_____

_____

JOKE CORNER

Where do the river people keep their money?

How do you communicate with a fish?

See page 26 for answers.

Mountains High

Graphs compare data. A bar graph uses bars to show data.
A line graph shows how data changes over time. Both types of graphs
use a scale to show the units used in the graph.

Use the chart to make a bar graph of the heights of famous mountain peaks.

1. A graph needs to have a title to tell what the graph is about.
   Write a title at the top of the graph.

2. Graphs also need labels to show what data is being shown. Write a label
   at the bottom of the graph.

Heights of Famous Mountains						
MOUNTAIN	Vesuvius	Mt. McKinley	Mt. Rainier	Mt. Everest	Kilimanjaro	Mt. St. Helens
HEIGHT IN FEET	4,190	20,320	14,410	29,028	19,340	8,364

3. Write a label on the left side of the graph.

4. Draw a bar to show the height of each mountain.

Title _____

```
30,000
25,000
20,000
15,000
10,000
 5,000
     0
        Vesuvius   Mt. McKinley   Mt Rainier   Mt. Everest   Kilimanjaro   Mt. St. Helens
```

_____

5. About how many times taller is the tallest mountain than the

   shortest mountain? _____

Many people have attempted to climb Mt. Everest, the world's tallest mountain. Although some have died, many have been successful in this dangerous quest. Use the data in the chart to make a line graph showing the number of people who reached the top of Mt. Everest between 1991 and 1997. We will use a line graph because we are showing change over time.

Number of People to Reach Top of Mt. Everest							
Year	1991	1992	1993	1994	1995	1996	1997
Number of people	38	90	129	51	83	98	85

6. Write a title for the graph.

7. Write one label below the graph and one on the left side of the graph.

8. Write a scale on the left side of the graph. Since the greatest number of people is 129, you should count by 10's when writing your scale. Your scale should start at 0.

9. Now that you have set up your graph, record the data found in the chart at the top of the page.

Title _____

    1991   1992   1993   1994   1995   1996   1997

_____

10. In which year did the most people reach the top of Mt. Everest? _____

Where in the World?

The world is full of places, some familiar and some not. A reference book, globe, or wise parent may be helpful in answering the questions.

1. It was here that the Declaration of Independence was adopted on July 4, 1776. _____

2. The Capitol building, the White House, and the Vietnam Memorial are here. _____

3. Minnesota's baseball team is the Twins, named after the twin cities. What two cities are known as the twin cities?

   _____

4. There is only one place in the United States where four states border each other. What are the four states?_____

   _____

5. Only three states form the west coast of the continental United States. What are the three states?_____

6. This is the coldest, most desolate region on earth. Summer temperatures average well below freezing here. _____

7. This Asian country contains the largest man-made object in the world. The object is even visible from outer space. _____

8. Mt. Everest is the highest mountain in the world. Between which two countries is it located? _____

9. Lake Victoria is the largest lake in Africa and the second largest freshwater lake in the world. In which three African countries does it lie?

   _____

Answers from page 23: In a river bank. You drop it a line.

SPORTS AND LEISURE

ANCIENT OLYMPIC GAMES

Millions of people all over the world watch the Olympics, either in person or on television. Perhaps no other event captures the imagination of so many people from such different cultures. The Olympics has been called "The Greatest Sporting Event in the World."

The Olympic Games may have begun as early as 1300 B.C. However, it was not until 776 B.C. that a written record was kept of the Olympics. Archaeologists have discovered ancient writings with references to Olympic winners. They have also found pieces from statues of ancient Olympic champions. And, they have found Olympic competitors pictured on ancient vases, cups, and bowls.

The first Olympic Games were part of a large religious festival held every four years in Olympia, Greece, to honor Zeus, the king of the Greek gods. At first, the Olympic Games involved only foot races. Later, events such as chariot races, horse races, and the pentathlon were added. The pentathlon was an event in which a single athlete would compete in five events: discus throw, long jump, javelin throw, upright wrestling, and footrace. For many years, the winner of the pentathlon was the most honored athlete in Greece.

Travelers from all over the ancient Greek world would flock to the Olympic Games. They came on foot, on horseback, in carriages, and on barges. Wars and skirmishes were common in the ancient world. However, during the Olympic Games, a sacred truce was declared. All weapons were forbidden in Olympia. Safe passage was guaranteed to all competitors and visitors. The truce lasted long enough to permit the competitors and spectators to travel to the Games, enjoy them, and travel home again.

Visiting Olympia during the ancient Games was evidently quite an experience. Visitors would tour the magnificent temple built to honor Zeus. They would also tour many other ornate buildings erected by the various Greek city-states to house their prize possessions and glorify their accomplishments.

Only first place winners were honored in the ancient Games. Winners would receive a wreath made from the branches of the sacred olive tree. They would also benefit from rewards such as good jobs and being excused from paying taxes.

The Olympic Games were banned by the Greek Emperor in A.D. 394 because he felt that the Games were corrupt. Also, the Games were centered on the worship of pagan gods, and this did not sit well with the Christian church. This ban ended an Olympic tradition that had lasted for over one thousand years. Olympia was abandoned. Earthquakes and floods erased the city that had housed the thousand-year-old event.

Draw a line under each correct answer or fill in each blank.

1. Much is known about the Olympic Games held between 1300 B.C. and 776 B.C.

    a. yes   **b.** no   **c.** doesn't say

2. Which of the following is not a source of knowledge of the ancient Games?

    a. ancient writings   **c.** old radio broadcasts

    b. broken statues   **d.** old vases and cups

3. In ancient Greece, the major reason for the Games was _____.

    a. to honor Zeus

    b. to show off athletes to other nations

    c. to earn money for the city-state

4. Which of the following is **not** part of the pentathlon?

    a. footrace   **c.** swimming

    b. wrestling   **d.** javelin throw

5. The Olympic Games ended in A.D. 394 because _____.

    a. the city-states were involved in too many wars

    b. the Games became too expensive for the poor nations

    c. the Christian emperor did not like that the Games were used to worship a pagan god

6. In the second paragraph, which word fits each definition?

   a. "people who study early human cultures" _____

   b. "persons in a contest" _____

7. In the fourth paragraph, which word fits each definition?

   a. " small fights" _____

   b. "an agreement to temporarily stop fighting" _____

   c. "persons who watch an event" _____

8. In the seventh paragraph, which word fits each definition?

   a. "customs passed down through generations" _____

   b. "in early Christian times, one who worshipped false gods"

      _____

   c. "dishonest" _____

9. Second place finishers in the ancient Games received huge silver trophies.

   a. yes   b. no   c. does not say

10. The olive tree was sacred in ancient Greece.

    a. yes   b. no   c. does not say

 If you have Internet access, you can read about the Olympics at www.olympic-usa.org.

Baseball Riddle

Two baseball teams played a game. One team won but no man touched the base. How could that be? To find the answer to the riddle, you must first solve the problems. Next, match your answers to the letters in the answer key and write the letters in the blanks .

1. 500
−225

2. 243
−132

3. 7.6
+5.4

4. 6009
−4502

5. $5.69
−2.40

6. 1261
+1091

7. 15.26
+ 2.74

8. 5607
−3255

9. 13.91
+ 2.09

10. 3.06
−8.94

11. 60)720

12. 5)40

13. 5)75

14. 9
× 2

15. 8)96

16. 13)169

17. 42
×56

18. 4)64

19. 5)510

20. 78
+305

ANSWER KEY

A = 16	G = 8	L = 12	R = 18	
B = 275	H = 1507	M = 102	S = 383	W = $3.29
E = 2352	I = 15	O = 111	T = 13	

ANSWER

B __ __ __ __   __ __ __ __   A __ __ __ __ __
1 2 3 4 5 6 7 8 9 10 11 12 13 14 15

__ __ __ __ __
16 17 18 19 20

Read About It During World War II, the ranks of the baseball leagues shrank as more and more players went off to war. The solution to keep fans coming to the parks? Women's professional baseball. Read all about it in *A Whole New Ball Game* by Sue Macy.

Olympic Geometry

Write the letter of the figure defined.

1. _____ *Point:* an exact location

2. _____ *Line:* a straight path that goes on forever in both directions

3. _____ *Line Segment:* a part of a line with 2 endpoints

4. _____ *Ray:* a part of a line with 1 endpoint

5. _____ *Intersecting Lines:* lines or line segments that cross at one point

6. _____ *Perpendicular Lines:* 2 intersecting lines that form right angles

7. _____ *Parallel Lines:* 2 lines on the same plane that never intersect

8. _____ *Right Angle:* 2 rays with common endpoint and an angle that is 90 degrees

9. _____ *Obtuse Angle:* 2 rays with common endpoint and an angle that is greater than 90 degrees

10. _____ *Acute Angle:* 2 rays with common endpoint and an angle that is less than 90 degrees

a.

b.

c.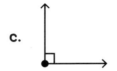

d.

e.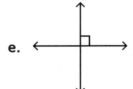

f. •

g.

h. •————————•

i.

j. ⟷
⟷

32

A polygon is a closed figure made with line segments. A polygon is named by the number of its sides. Draw the appropriate polygon below.

11. 3 sides   triangle

12. 4 sides   quadrilateral

13. 5 sides   pentagon

14. 6 sides   hexagon

15. 8 sides   octagon

There are many kinds of quadrilaterals (four-sided polygons). Some of them have special features. Use these definitions to help you name the quadrilaterals below.

Rectangle: two pairs of congruent, parallel sides; four right angles

Square: all sides are parallel and congruent; four right angles

Parallelogram: two pairs of parallel and congruent sides

Rhombus: all sides are parallel and congruent

Trapezoid: only two sides parallel and congruent

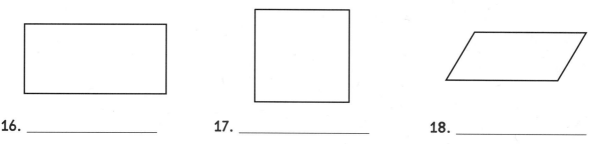

16. _____   **17.** _____   **18.** _____

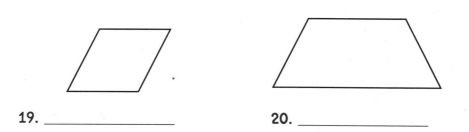

19. _____   **20.** _____

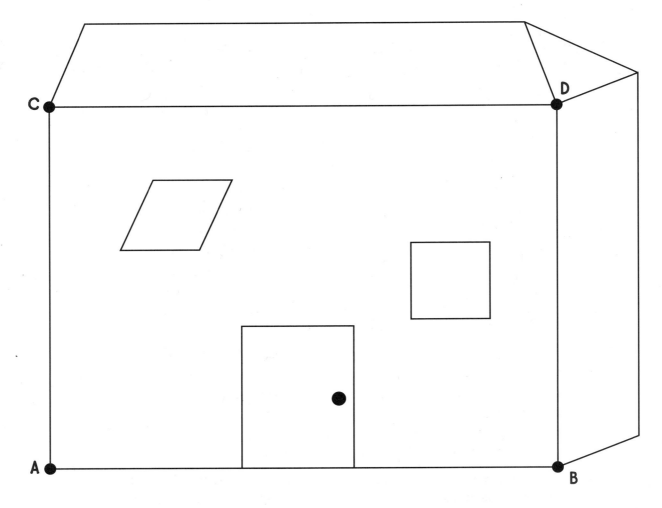

Use the picture of the house above to follow these directions.

21. Color the square window green.

22. Color the rhombus window yellow.

23. What polygon is the shape of the door? _____

24. Name the 2 parallel line segments (Line segments are named using their

    endpoints. Example: AB)_____ ___

25. Name 2 perpendicular line segments. _____

26. Use a red marker to trace a right angle.

27. Use an orange marker to trace an acute angle.

28. Use a red marker to trace an obtuse angle.

29. Color a triangle blue.

30. Color a trapezoid purple.

31. What is the doorknob? _____

32. Color a parallelogram brown.

Modern Olympic Games

As you learned earlier, the ancient Olympic Games lasted over 1000 years until they were stopped in 394 by a Greek emperor. Olympia was abandoned. This is the story of how the modern Olympic Games rose from the ashes of the ancient Olympic Games.

For 1400 years, Olympia lay buried under mud. Finally, in the nineteenth century, archaeologists began to explore and unearth the remains of the ancient Olympic site at Olympia. This led to renewed interest in the Olympics. The first modern Olympic Games were held in 1896 in Athens, the capital of Greece. Today, the Olympics take place every four years. Each four-year period is called an Olympiad.

At first, there were only Summer Olympics. In 1924, the Winter Olympics were added. Some of the sports included in the Summer Olympics are track and field, basketball, boxing, field hockey, equestrian sports, cycling, gymnastics, swimming and yachting. The Winter Olympics includes such sports as figure skating, ice hockey, ski jumping, speed skating, and the luge.

There are many important traditions of the modern Olympics. Perhaps the best known tradition is the Olympic flag, which has five rings colored blue, yellow, black, green, and red. The rings are linked together as a symbol of world friendship. Another important tradition is the Olympic flame. The Olympic flame is carried from Olympia by a relay of runners into the Olympic stadium where the Olympic torch is lit. The torch burns until the Games end. A third important tradition of the Olympics is the Olympic hymn. And, there is an Olympic oath that is pronounced by a contestant from the host country on behalf of all of the athletes taking part in the games.

~1896~
FIRST MODERN OLYMPIC

~1900~
WOMEN ALLOWED TO COMPETE

Unfortunately, the ancient tradition of the truce did not carry forward to modern times, and the modern Olympics are threatened by politics. There are many examples of politics affecting the Olympics. For example, the Olympics were not held during the World Wars of 1914-1918 and 1939-1945. After each World War, some nations were not invited to participate. In 1972, in the host city Munich, Arab terrorists attacked the Olympic village and killed 11 Israeli athletes. In 1980, the United States, Germany and Japan did not participate in the Summer Games in Moscow to protest the Russian invasion of Afghanistan. In 1984, the Communist countries boycotted the Summer Games in Los Angeles, fearing that their athletes would not be protected.

The Olympics have changed considerably since ancient times. For instance, women were not permitted to compete in the ancient games. In the 1900 Olympics in Paris, women competed in a few events for the first time. Today, women compete in most of the events.

The Olympics have grown considerably. At the ancient Olympic Games in Athens in 1896, there were 8 nations competing in 10 sports and 42 events. In the 1996 Summer Games in Atlanta there were over 15,000 athletes, coaches, and officials from over 200 nations competing in almost 30 sports and 300 events.

Despite political problems, the athletes of the Olympics make friends from all over the world. At least a part of the Olympic dream of promoting understanding among peoples of the world is achieved.

~1924~
WINTER OLYMPICS ADDED.

~1984~
COMMUNIST COUNTRIES
BOYCOTT

Draw a line under each right answer or fill in each blank.

1. Women have always been an important part of the Olympics.

   a. yes   **b.** no   **c.** does not say

2. Give an example of politics affecting the Olympic Games.

   _____

3. Which of the following does not take place in the Summer Olympics?

   a. boxing   **c.** the luge

   b. cycling   **d.** gymnastics

4. Name three important Olympic traditions. _____

   _____   _____

5. What word in the fourth to last paragraph means "refused to participate"?

   _____

6. In the last paragraph, the article says that the goal of the Olympics
   is to promote understanding among peoples of the world. Do you think
   an athletic event like the Olympics can do that? Why or why not? Be sure
   to include a topic sentence, at least three supporting details, a good
   transition, and a conclusion.

   _____

   _____

   _____

   _____

   _____

   _____

   _____

 **Read About It** What does it take to be a champion? Read about the lives of ten inspirational men and women of sports in *Champions* by Bill Littlefield.

High-Flying Fractions

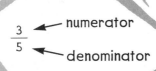

$\dfrac{3}{5}$ ← numerator
← denominator

A mixed fraction has a whole number and fractional part. $7\dfrac{3}{4}$

An improper fraction has a numerator greater than or equal to the denominator. $\dfrac{12}{2}$

Write each improper fraction as a whole or mixed number.

1. $\dfrac{9}{8}$

2. $\dfrac{10}{5}$

3. $\dfrac{10}{4}$

4. $\dfrac{23}{3}$

5. $\dfrac{9}{2}$

6. $\dfrac{25}{5}$

Write each mixed number as an improper fraction.

7. $2\dfrac{5}{6}$

8. $4\dfrac{2}{5}$

9. $3\dfrac{3}{7}$

10. $12\dfrac{1}{2}$

11. $7\dfrac{3}{6}$

12. $9\dfrac{1}{3}$

13. Write the number 4 as an improper fraction with a denominator of 2. _____

14. Write the number 9 as an improper fraction with a denominator of 3. _____

15. If you had only a $\dfrac{1}{3}$-cup measuring cup, how many times would you have to fill it to measure $3\dfrac{2}{3}$ cups of oatmeal? _____

Kites are more than 2500 years old. Before there was string, people would use a vine to fly their kites. Kites have had many uses in history. They have carried burning bombs, flown spies over enemy territory, and carried special weather instruments into the sky.

Making Music

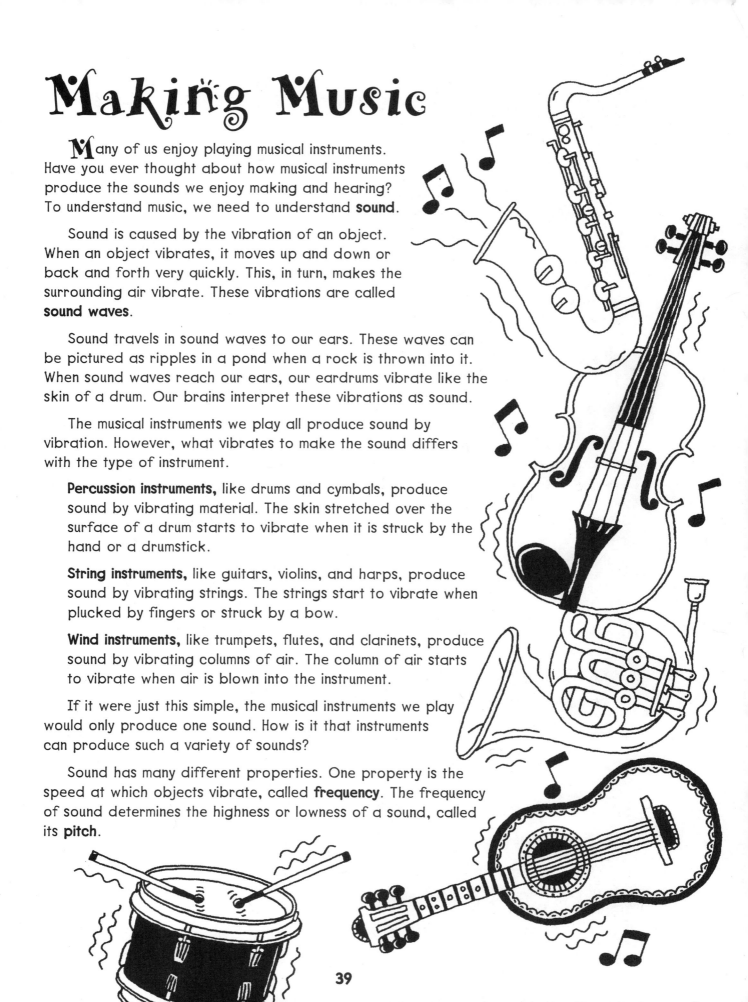

Many of us enjoy playing musical instruments. Have you ever thought about how musical instruments produce the sounds we enjoy making and hearing? To understand music, we need to understand **sound**.

Sound is caused by the vibration of an object. When an object vibrates, it moves up and down or back and forth very quickly. This, in turn, makes the surrounding air vibrate. These vibrations are called **sound waves**.

Sound travels in sound waves to our ears. These waves can be pictured as ripples in a pond when a rock is thrown into it. When sound waves reach our ears, our eardrums vibrate like the skin of a drum. Our brains interpret these vibrations as sound.

The musical instruments we play all produce sound by vibration. However, what vibrates to make the sound differs with the type of instrument.

Percussion instruments, like drums and cymbals, produce sound by vibrating material. The skin stretched over the surface of a drum starts to vibrate when it is struck by the hand or a drumstick.

String instruments, like guitars, violins, and harps, produce sound by vibrating strings. The strings start to vibrate when plucked by fingers or struck by a bow.

Wind instruments, like trumpets, flutes, and clarinets, produce sound by vibrating columns of air. The column of air starts to vibrate when air is blown into the instrument.

If it were just this simple, the musical instruments we play would only produce one sound. How is it that instruments can produce such a variety of sounds?

Sound has many different properties. One property is the speed at which objects vibrate, called **frequency**. The frequency of sound determines the highness or lowness of a sound, called its **pitch**.

When an object vibrates slowly, it produces long sound waves with peaks that are far apart. Long sound waves have a low frequency and low pitch.

Long sound wave: low frequency, low pitch

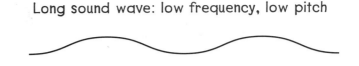

When an object vibrates fast, it produces short sound waves with peaks that are close together. Short sound waves have a high frequency and high pitch.

Short sound wave: high frequency, high pitch

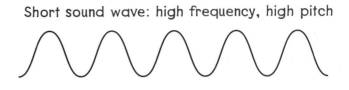

When you hear an orchestra play, you hear a seemingly endless variety of sounds as musical instruments produce different frequencies. Along with pitch, musicians control the volume, the length, and the quality of sound to create the beautiful music we enjoy.

Fill in the blank or circle the correct answer.

1. The main idea of this passage is that _____.

   a. orchestras make beautiful sounds

   b. sound is caused by vibration

   c. there are three types of musical instruments

2. Mark these sentences true or false.

   _____ Musical instruments produce sound by vibration.

   _____ Slow vibrations produce sounds with low pitch.

   _____ In percussion, string, and wind instruments, a flap of metal vibrates to produce sound.

3. Although not directly stated in this passage, you can tell that _____.

    a. frequency is the speed at which objects vibrate

    b. the science of sound is very important to musicians

    c. sound waves are exactly like light waves

4. The word **it** in the second to last paragraph, first sentence, refers to

_____.

5. A musician controls the pitch, the volume, the length, and the quality of sound.

    a. yes   **b.** no   **c.** does not say

Solve these problems.

6. 402 × 7
7. 7134 × 5
8. 462 × 3
9. 577 × 2
10. 310 × 6

11. 6028 × 13
12. 12 × 16
13. $20.44 × 3
14. 83 × 17
15. $52.47 × 7

JOKE CORNER

Why is it so hot in a stadium after a baseball game?

Why does it take longer to run from second base to third base than from first to second?

Answer on page 46.

Exercise Your Mind

A solid figure is made up of plane figure faces, edges where those faces meet, and vertices where points are formed. Label each figure below.

rectangular prism   sphere   cone   cylinder   pyramid   cube

  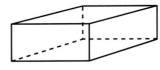

1. _____ Sphere _____   2. _____ Cube _____   3. _____ rectangle _____

4. _____ a Pyramid _____   5. _____ cone _____   6. _____ cylinder _____

7. The face of a cube is a _____ square _____.

8. The flat face of a cone is a _____ circle _____.

9. The face of a rectangular prism is a _____.

What am I?

10. I have 6 faces all the same size and shape. _____

11. I have no faces. _____

12. I have 2 circular faces. _____

13. I have 4 triangular faces and one rectangular face. _____

Compute these distances.

14.   10 feet 2 inches
     − 8 feet 8 inches

15.   2 yards 2 feet
     + 3 yards 2 feet

Marble Math

Fractions that name the same amount are called equivalent fractions.

$$\frac{1}{2} \quad = \quad \frac{5}{10} \quad = \quad \frac{16}{32} \quad = \quad \frac{50}{100}$$

Multiply or divide to find the equivalent fraction.

Example: $\frac{2}{3} \xrightarrow{\times 2} = \frac{4}{6} \xleftarrow{\times 2}$ $\qquad$ $\frac{12}{18} \xrightarrow{\div 6} = \frac{2}{3} \xleftarrow{\div 6}$

1. $\frac{3}{4}$ $\qquad$ 2. $\frac{1}{3}$ $\qquad$ 3. $\frac{12}{15}$

4. $\frac{5}{6}$ $\qquad$ 5. $\frac{4}{8}$ $\qquad$ 6. $\frac{9}{32}$

Reducing a fraction to its simplest form means when the numerator and denominator have no common factors other than 1.

Example: $\frac{12}{36} \xrightarrow{\div 2} = \frac{6}{18} \xrightarrow{\div 6} = \frac{1}{3}$ simplest form

Write each fraction in its simplest form.

7. $\frac{4}{6}$ $\qquad$ 8. $\frac{6}{15}$ $\qquad$ 9. $\frac{8}{10}$

10. $\frac{3}{24}$ $\qquad$ 11. $\frac{12}{16}$ $\qquad$ 12. $\frac{11}{22}$

13. $\frac{3}{9}$ $\qquad$ 14. $\frac{21}{30}$ $\qquad$ 15. $\frac{15}{60}$

 DO YOU KNOW Marbles can be made from many materials such as glass, stone, and plastic. Perhaps the most unusual ones are used by some children in Turkey and Iran. They are made with the knucklebones of sheep!

Music to My Ears

The science of sound is essential to making music. Let's explore musical sound by making some instruments.

Make a drum

What you will need

Empty coffee can
Balloon
Rubber band
Spoon

Instructions

- Cut the neck off the balloon. Cut the balloon in half and stretch it over the open end of the coffee can.

- Stretch the rubber band around the can's open end to hold the balloon in place.

- Tap the balloon drumhead with the spoon.

- Pull the balloon tighter over the can's open end. Tap the balloon drumhead with the spoon.

Fill in the blanks.

1. What is vibrating to produce the sound you hear?

   _____

2. Which produced a higher sound, the looser or the tighter drumhead?

   _____

3. Which was vibrating faster, the looser or the tighter drumhead?

   _____

4. Based on what you learned in your experiment, describe the difference in sound between a snare drum and a kettledrum, or timpani.

   _____

   _____

Make a wind instrument

What you will need

4 identical bottles, such as soda or small juice bottles

Instructions

- Line up the bottles in a row.
- Leave the first bottle empty. Fill the second bottle one quarter full, the third bottle half full, and the fourth bottle three quarters full.
- Blow across—not into—the mouths of the bottles to create sounds.

Circle the correct answer.

1. Which bottle produces the lowest sound?

    a. the bottle with the least amount of water and most amount of air

    b. the bottle with the most amount of water and least amount of air

2. Which bottle produces the highest sound?

    a. the bottle with the least amount of water and most amount of air

    b. the bottle with the most amount of water and least amount of air

When you blow across the bottle, the air vibrates. In the bottle with no water, there is more air and the speed of vibration is slower. Therefore, the pitch is low. In the bottle with the most water, there is less air and the speed of vibration is faster. Therefore, the pitch is higher.

FACTOR TREES

Find the prime factors in the numbers below by drawing a factor tree.

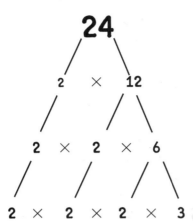

24
```
        24
       /  \
      2  ×  12
     /      / \
    2  ×  2  ×  6
   /      /    / \
  2  ×  2  ×  2  ×  3
```

12

36

48

27

81

Solve these problems.

1. $6.2 + 9.1 =$

2. $23.75 - 14.21 =$

3. $32.67 - 13.09 =$

4. $60.03 + 21.74 =$

Solve these problems in your head.

5. $6.2 + 6.2 + 6.3 =$

6. $9.3 + 9.2 + 10 =$

7. $2.5 + 3.5 =$

8. $400 \times 70 =$

Because there's a shortstop in between.
All the fans have left.
Answers from page 41:

46

Our Changing Weather

One thing we know about the weather is that it's always changing. One day might be sunny and warm, and the next day might be rainy and windy. What causes such striking changes in our weather?

Weather is the condition of the air that surrounds the earth. It includes temperature, air pressure, wind, and humidity (the amount of water vapor in the air).

Changes in our weather are caused by the movement of large bodies of air called **air masses**. Air masses form over areas where the temperature does not change, such as the North Pole, the South Pole, and the equator. Air masses take on the temperature and humidity of the area over which they form. Consequently, an air mass that forms over the North Pole or South Pole is cold and heavy, while an air mass that forms over the equator is warm and light.

Air masses are constantly moving between the poles and the equator. The heavier cold air from the poles moves toward the equator, while the lighter warm air above the equator rises and moves toward the poles. This movement of air is called wind.

What did you just read? Circle the correct answer or fill in the blank.

1. Which is **not** included in the definition of weather?
   a. temperature
   b. air pressure
   c. wind
   d. humidity
   e. ground

2. Changes in the weather are caused by _____.
   a. the North and South Poles
   b. movement of air masses
   c. changes in temperature

3. Air masses form over the equator and the North and South Poles because _____.
   a. cold air is heavier than warm air
   b. warm air moves toward the poles
   c. the temperature in these areas is either constantly cold or hot

4. Movement of air is called _____.

When a cold air mass meets a warm air mass, the two air masses do not mix together. Instead they form a battle line called a **front**. When a front and its accompanying air mass passes over a region, the weather of that region changes.

There are two main types of fronts, **warm fronts** and **cold fronts**. Whether a front is cold or warm depends on whether the cold air mass or the warm air mass is winning the battle. When fronts battle, clouds usually appear and we are likely to have rain or snow.

A **cold front** occurs when a cold air mass moves under a warm air mass and pushes the warm air up. The cold air mass replaces the warm air at ground level. Cold fronts can cause sudden changes in the weather. After a cold front passes through, the temperature drops and the skies clear.

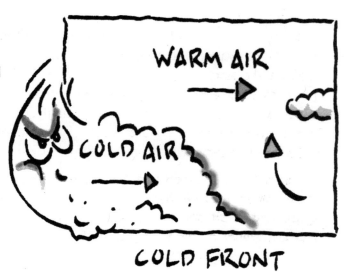

COLD FRONT

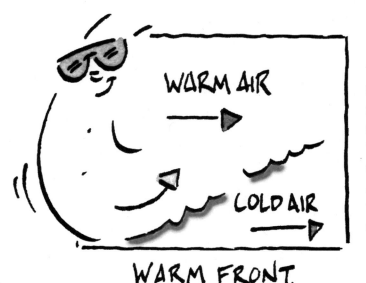

WARM FRONT.

A **warm front** occurs when a warm air mass moves over a retreating cold air mass. The warm air front gradually replaces the cold air front at ground level. Warm fronts move slower than cold fronts and the weather change is less sudden. After a warm front passes through, the temperature rises sharply, the skies clear, and the humidity increases.

Each day our lives are influenced by what the weather will be. Should we plan a picnic in the park or should we plan a trip to a museum? If the weather isn't what we hoped for today, we know there's a good chance it will be different tomorrow.

Answer these questions about what you just read.
Circle the correct answer or fill in the blank.

1. When a front passes through a region, the weather _____.
   a. stays the same
   b. changes
   c. does not say

2. Which two sentences are not true?
   a. Warm air masses and cold air masses mix together.
   b. There are two main types of fronts.
   c. Cold fronts cause sudden changes in weather.
   d. Warm fronts move faster than cold fronts.

3. Warm fronts are followed by a rise in temperature.
   a. yes
   b. no
   c. does not say

4. If a front is like a battle line, what are the two enemies?

   _____

   _____

Weather
Whether the weather be fine
Or whether the weather be not,
Whether the weather be cold
Or whether the weather be not,
We'll weather the weather
Whatever the weather
Whether we like it or not.
Anonymous

A Drop of Fractions

Calculate the following.

Example: $\frac{3}{5}$ of 10 = 6

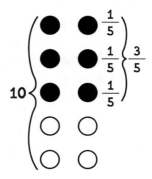

10	÷	5	=	2		2	×	3	=	6
total in set		number of groups	quotient			quotient		number of groups		answer

1. $\frac{2}{4}$ of 20 =

2. $\frac{2}{9}$ of 27 =

3. $\frac{1}{2}$ of 20 =

4. $\frac{2}{3}$ of 24 =

5. $\frac{3}{8}$ of 16 =

6. $\frac{2}{3}$ of 18 =

7. Lauren, Kristin, and Kelly are making fruit salad. Lauren starts with $2\frac{1}{2}$ pounds of watermelon. Kristin adds $1\frac{2}{3}$ pounds of grapes. Kelly throw in $1\frac{2}{6}$ pounds of strawberries. How much does the fruit salad weigh? _____

8. There were 36 animals in the zoo. One-half were monkeys. One-third were birds. How many were not monkeys or birds? _____

9. Design a flag that is $\frac{1}{2}$ red, $\frac{2}{8}$ green, $\frac{1}{8}$ yellow, and $\frac{1}{8}$ blue.

Read About It Sometimes the weather can have disastrous results. A large dam burst after unusually heavy rains, causing a 40-foot high wave of water to crash through Johnstown, Pennsylvania, in May 1889. Read about the famous and tragic Johnstown flood in *Head for the Hills!* by Paul Robert Walker.

Windy Poetry

Look at the two poems below. The first poem is the real version. It is written in the present tense, as if the action is taking place today. Let's change the poem to the past tense, as if the action took place yesterday. To do this, change the underlined verbs in the first poem from the present to the past tense and write them in the blanks in the second poem.

The March Wind
Anonymous

(Present Tense)

I <u>come</u> to work as well as play;

   I'll <u>tell</u> you what I <u>do</u>;

I <u>whistle</u> all the live-long day,

   "Woo-oo-oo-oo! Woo-oo!"

I <u>toss</u> the branches up and down

   And <u>shake</u> them to and fro,

I <u>whirl</u> the leaves in flocks of brown

   And <u>send</u> them high and low.

I <u>strew</u> the twigs upon the ground,

   The frozen earth I <u>sweep</u>;

I <u>blow</u> the children round and round

   And <u>wake</u> the flowers from sleep.

(Past Tense)

I <u>came</u> to work as well as play;

   I _____ **you** what I _____

I _____ all the live-long day,

   "Woo-oo-oo-oo! **Woo-oo!**"

I _____ the **branches** up and down

   And _____ them to **and** fro,

I _____ the leaves in flocks of brown

   And _____ them high and low.

I <u>strew</u> the twigs **upon** the ground,

   The **frozen** earth I _____;

I _____ the children **round** and round

   And _____ the flowers from sleep.

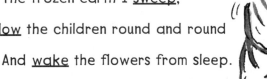

52

1. "The March Wind" is a wintry poem. When reading this poem, you can picture a cold March day. In the space below, write two lines from "The March Wind" that make you think of winter.

_____

_____

2. Which line of "The March Wind" makes the reader think that spring is coming?

_____

3. Who is the "I" in the poem? _____

This poem uses personification, which means describing nonhuman things as people. For example, the poet says the wind "comes to work as well as play." Could the wind really do that? Of course not! The poet is describing the wind as a person.

4. Write two other lines from "The March Wind" that describe the wind as a person.

_____

_____

There are eight parts of speech: **verb, noun, adjective, adverb, pronoun, conjunction, preposition,** and **interjection.**

You already know the verbs in "The March Wind." Now look at the bold words in the second version of "The March Wind" and write them next to their parts of speech. You should find at least one of each.

5. **Noun** (a person, place, or thing) _____

6. **Adjective** (describes a noun) _____

7. **Adverb** (describes a verb, an adjective, or another adverb) _____

8. **Pronoun** (stands for a noun) _____

9. **Conjunction** (a connecting word) _____

10. **Preposition** (relates things to each other) _____

11. **Interjection** (an exclamation) _____

Put On Your Poet's Hat

When you write a poem, you need to create a word picture of your topic. Start by picturing your topic in your mind. Brainstorm, thinking about the sights, sounds, smells, and feelings associated with your topic. Write down words and phrases that come to mind as you think about your topic. For example, think about the summer breeze. Here are some words and phases that describe a summer breeze:

soft

gentle

ruffles my hair

cools my skin

refreshing

feathery

sings me to sleep

We can create a simple poem out of these words and phrases.

Soft as a feather
The summer breeze
Ruffles my hair and
Sings me to sleep.

Now it's your turn. Picture a violent thunderstorm with lightning flashing and thunder crashing. Brainstorm. Write down all the words and phrases that come to you as you picture the fierce storm.

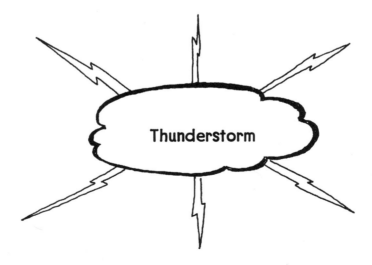

Thunderstorm

On the next page, write a simple poem that creates a picture and illustrate it.

My Poem

SMELLS feelings Sounds SIGHTS

Illustrate your poem in the frame below.

WEATHER MATH

The newspaper prints information about the weather every day.
Use the following information from the weather section of a newspaper
to answer the questions.

		Yesterday's barometer readings Philadelphia, PA		Yesterday's High Temperature Readings U.S. Cities	
Sunrise	6:30 a.m.	6 a.m.	30.00		
Sunset	7:31 p.m.	Noon	30.05	Seattle	82°
Moonrise	5:00 p.m.	6 p.m.	30.11	Denver	85°
Moonset	2:11 a.m.	10 p.m.	30.06	Los Angeles	96°
		Midnight	30.08	Boston	76°
				Memphis	86°

1. What is the difference in hours and minutes between sunrise and sunset? _____

2. What is the difference in hours and minutes between moonrise

    and moonset? _____

3. If your mother tells you that you should go to bed

    at $4\frac{1}{2}$ hours after moonrise, what time would that be?

    _____

4. Write the noon barometer reading in word form.

    _____

5. Write a number that comes between 30.08

    and 30.11. _____

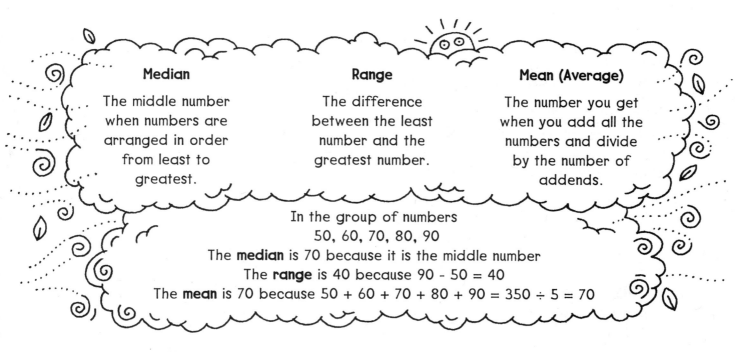

Median

The middle number when numbers are arranged in order from least to greatest.

Range

The difference between the least number and the greatest number.

Mean (Average)

The number you get when you add all the numbers and divide by the number of addends.

In the group of numbers
50, 60, 70, 80, 90
The **median** is 70 because it is the middle number
The **range** is 40 because 90 - 50 = 40
The **mean** is 70 because 50 + 60 + 70 + 80 + 90 = 350 ÷ 5 = 70

Use the definitions at the top of this page and newspaper information on the previous page to answer the following questions.

Median: To find the median, first put your group of numbers in order.

6. Write yesterday's barometer readings in order from least to greatest.

   _____ _____ _____ _____ _____

   Write yesterday's temperature readings in order from least to greatest.

   _____ _____ _____ _____ _____

7. What is the median barometer reading? _____

8. What is the median temperature reading? _____

Range: To find the range, subtract the least number in the list from the greatest number in the list.

9. What is the range of barometer readings? _____

10. What is the range of temperature readings? _____

Mean: To find the mean, add all the numbers in the list and divide by the number of addends.

11. What is mean barometer reading? _____

12. What is the mean temperature reading? _____

The costliest hurricane in U.S. history was Hurricane Andrew in 1992, which caused about $20 billion in damages.

Let's suppose the exact number was $20,157,982,500.

13. In the number 20,157,982,500 how many

hundreds are there? _____

tens are there? _____

thousands are there? _____

ten thousands are there? _____

hundred thousands are there? _____

14. Round the number of 20,157,982,500 to

the nearest thousand _____

the nearest million _____

the nearest billion _____

The atmospheric pressure at sea level is 29.92 inches. A higher barometer reading means a high-pressure area is present, and the weather will be cool and clear. A lower reading indicates a low-pressure area, which means clouds and maybe a storm. The lowest air pressure on record was approximately 25.69 inches during a typhoon in the Philippine Sea on October 12, 1979.

How's the Weather?

Weather at noon today and forecasted high/low temperatures

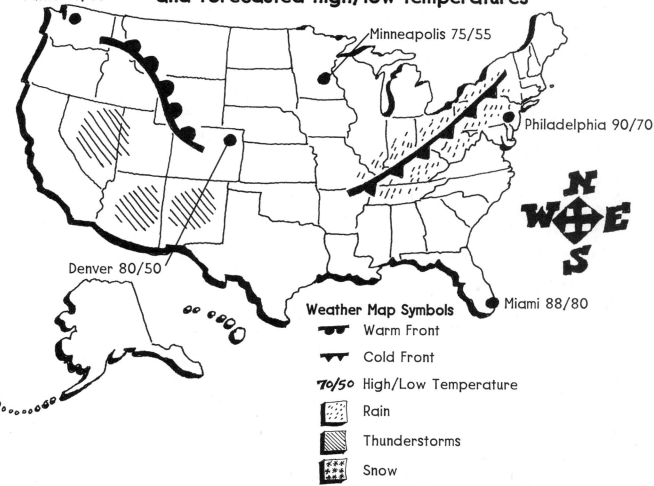

Seattle 70/53

Minneapolis 75/55

Philadelphia 90/70

Denver 80/50

Miami 88/80

Weather Map Symbols

Warm Front

Cold Front

70/50 High/Low Temperature

Rain

Thunderstorms

Snow

Newspapers publish weather forecasts in the weather section of the paper. Above is a weather map you might find in your newspaper. Use it to answer the following questions.

1. Look at the heading for the weather map. This map forecasts or predicts today's weather for what time of day?

   _____

2. What do the lines with the triangles show?  _____

   What do the lines with the semicircles show? _____

3. The triangles and semicircles are pointed in the direction that the front is moving. Which direction is the warm front moving, to the east or to the west? _____ Which direction is the cold front moving, to the north or to the south? _____

4. What city has the highest temperature? _____

   What city has the lowest temperature? _____

   What city has the biggest difference between its high and low temperature?

   _____

5. In which part of the country is it raining?

   a. northeast   **c.** midwest

   b. south   **d.** none

6. In which part of the country are there thunderstorms?

   a. northeast   **c.** southwest

   b. north   **d.** none

7. In which part of the country is there snow?

   a. southeast   **c.** east

   b. west   **d.** none

8. Our weather moves from west to east. Therefore, if it's cold in Colorado on Wednesday, it could get cold in Ohio on Thursday. Locate Philadelphia on the map. If you live in Philadelphia, what do you think the weather might be in the next couple days?

   _____

   _____

9. Locate Minneapolis on the map. What weather might Minneapolis expect in the next day or two?

   _____

   _____

"Weather" You Like It or Not

FACTS

Perimeter is the distance around a figure

Area is the number of square units it takes to cover the surface of a plane figure (length × width)

Find the perimeter of these figures.

1.
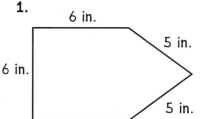
6 in.
5 in.
6 in.
5 in.
6 in.

_____

2.
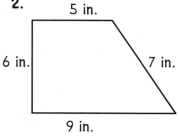
5 in.
6 in.
7 in.
9 in.

_____

3.
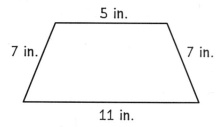
5 in.
7 in.
7 in.
11 in.

_____

Find the perimeter and area of the following.

4.
7 in.
2 in.

perimeter = _____

area = _____

5.
6 in.
3 in.

perimeter = _____

area = _____

6. A rectangle whose
length = 6 inches
width = 4 inches

perimeter = _____

area = _____

7. A square whose
sides = 9 inches

perimeter = _____

area = _____

8. One side of a square box is $\frac{1}{4}$ foot. What is the perimeter of the box?

_____

9. The Smith family is building a dog pen 10 feet long by 8 feet wide. What is the perimeter of the pen? What is the area?

perimeter = _____ feet

area = _____ square feet

FACTS

Volume is the number of cubic units needed to fill a solid
(length × width × height)

Find the volume of the rectangular prisms whose measurements are in inches.

10.

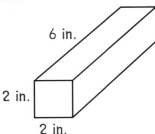

6 in.

2 in.

2 in.

_____ cubic inches

11.

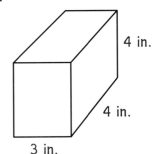

4 in.

4 in.

3 in.

_____ cubic inches

12.

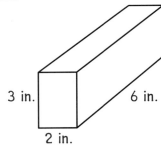

3 in.

6 in.

2 in.

_____ cubic inches

13. What is the volume of rectangular prism with a length of 5 inches,
a width of 3 inches, and a height of 4 inches.

_____ cubic inches

14. The Wilson's swimming pool is 28 feet long by 20 feet wide
by 11 feet deep. How much water is needed to fill the pool to the top?

_____ cubic feet

15. The area of a rectangle is 24 inches. Its length is 8 inches. What is its width?

_____ inches

If its height is 2 inches, what is its volume?

_____ cubic inches

JOKE CORNER

What's worse than raining cats and dogs?

What did the dirt say to the rain?

Answers on page 69.

Great Whirling Winds

Insert the correct punctuation in the following sentences. The number
of punctuation marks needed for each sentence is shown in parentheses.
The first one has been done for you.

1. Hurricanes are big⋀whirling storms that form over an ocean⊙ (2)

2. Hurricanes start out as tropical storms but they become hurricanes
   when their winds reach 75 miles per hour (2)

3. In other parts of the world hurricanes are called typhoons cyclones
   and willy-willies (4)

4. Hurricanes occur most often in the states of Texas Florida and Louisiana (3)

5. Over 6000 people were killed when a hurricane struck Galveston Texas,
   on August 27 1900 (4)

6. The U S National Weather Service an agency of the federal government
   started naming hurricanes in 1953 (5)

7. Hurricanes are given people's names in the order of the alphabet
   Abby Bob Cathy Danny Elizabeth Frank and so on (9)

8. Mom have you ever heard of a hurricane named Zelda asked Becky (5)

9. Goodness me I never have replied her mother (5)

Bonus questions:

10. Other than alphabetical order, what do you notice about the names
    used for hurricanes?

    _____

11. The letters Q, U, X, Y, and Z are not used in naming hurricanes.
    Can you guess why not?

    _____

A STORM OF MATH

To order fractions, change all fractions to a common denominator.

Example: $\frac{1}{2}$ $<$ $\frac{2}{3}$ $\frac{1}{2} = \frac{1\times 3}{2\times 3} = \boxed{\frac{3}{6}}$ $\frac{2}{3} = \frac{2\times 2}{2\times 3} = \boxed{\frac{4}{6}}$

Write $<$, $>$, or $=$.

1. $\frac{4}{9}$ ◯ $\frac{5}{9}$

2. $\frac{2}{3}$ ◯ $\frac{4}{9}$

3. $\frac{7}{12}$ ◯ $\frac{2}{6}$

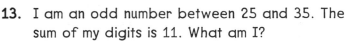

4. $\frac{6}{9}$ $4\frac{2}{3}$ ◯

5.

$\frac{1}{3}$ ◯ $\frac{4}{5}$

6. $\frac{3}{4}$ ◯ $\frac{3}{16}$

Fill in the missing numerators or denominators.

7. $\frac{2}{5} = \frac{}{15}$

8. $\frac{1}{4} = \frac{3}{}$

9. $\frac{3}{} = \frac{15}{5}$

10. $\frac{5}{9} = \frac{10}{}$

11. $\frac{2}{7} = \frac{8}{}$

12. $\frac{20}{} = \frac{2}{30}$

13. I am an odd number between 25 and 35. The sum of my digits is 11. What am I?

_____

14. I am a fraction with the numerator equal to the number of inches in a foot and the denominator equal to the numerator plus six. What am I?

_____

Round each decimal to the nearest whole number.

15. 50.5 = _____

16. 7.3 = _____

17. 600.2 = _____

18. 14.72 = _____

19. 6.81 = _____

20. 9.45 = _____

64

Predicting Weather Changes

Meteorologists use sophisticated equipment, such as barometers, to predict the weather. Barometers detect changes in the air pressure around us. Air pressure is the weight of the air pressing down on earth. Change in the air pressure can signal an upcoming change in the weather.

You can become a weather forecaster by making your own barometer and recording changes in the air pressure.

What you will need

Large jar such as a 32-ounce mayonnaise jar
Balloon
Rubber band
Drinking straw
Masking or transparent tape
Piece of paper
Pencil or pen

Instructions

1. Cut the neck off the balloon. Cut the balloon in half and stretch it tightly over the mouth of the jar. Hold the balloon in place with the rubber band.

2. Place the straw on the top of the jar so that one end of the straw is in the middle of the jar and one end hangs over the side. Tape the end of the straw to the balloon.

3. Tape the paper on a wall and put the jar in front of it. On the paper, write the word "low" at a spot near the top of the bottle and "high" about 2 inches above.

4. For the next seven days, mark the position of the straw on the paper. Observe the weather conditions outside.

5. Record your data on the chart on the next page.

6. As a check, find the actual barometer reading for the previous day in your newspaper. Record it on your chart.

Day of the Week	Straw Position (Higher, lower, or no change)	Weather Conditions (Choose from list)	Barometer Reading

Weather Descriptions

sunny & clear

partly cloudy

cloudy

showers

thunderstorms

rain

snow

1. What kind of weather did you observe when the straw was at its highest?

_____

2. What kind of weather did you observe when the straw was at its lowest?

_____

When the straw moves up, it means that the air pressure is rising. High air pressure usually means that the weather is clear. When the straw moves down, it means that the air pressure is falling. Low air pressure usually means that the weather is cloudy or rainy.

3. Does your data prove this? _____ Explain _____

_____

Bonus question:

4. How do you think your barometer works? For a clue, push down on the balloon with your finger and see what the straw does.

_____

_____

 DO YOU KNOW? Frogs love damp, humid conditions. Since the air becomes more humid before a rainstorm, expect to see more frogs around right before a rainstorm. Check it out the next time rain is forecast!

Weather News

Perhaps the most common topic of news is the weather. Almost every day, there are articles in the newspaper about how weather has created an extraordinary situation: a forest fire caused by drought, a church steeple tumbling to the ground after being hit by lightning, or a snowstorm that has closed schools.

1. Find an article in your newspaper that describes an event that is connected to the weather. We are going to use your article to learn how reporters write their stories.

Well-written newspaper articles answer five questions, known as the Five W's—

who   what   where   when   why

Reporters are taught to answer the Five W's very quickly at the beginning of their articles. After briefly covering these questions in the first paragraph or two, they go on to provide details in the rest of the article.

2. Read the first couple of paragraphs of your article and answer the following:

Who is the article about? _____

_____

What is the article about? _____

_____

Where does the story take place? _____

_____

When does the story take place? _____

_____

Why is this story important? _____

_____

3. How much of your article did you have to read to answer the 5 W's questions? Draw a line in your article to show how much you had to read to find the answers. Did you read one paragraph? Two? Half the article? The entire article?

_____

4. Now read the rest of the article. Write two facts you read that made the article more interesting but were not necessary to answer the Five W's.

Fact 1. _____

_____

Fact 2. _____

_____

You use the 5 W's when you write stories or research papers. You can even use it to write poetry. Let's write a poem answering the Five W's. The first line of the poem will answer "who," the second line "what," and so on. An example is given.

The snowman	who)
Had had better days	(what)
In my backyard	(where)
Than this bright, sunny February day	(when)
When he lost his body mass really fast!	(why)

Now it's your turn to write a poem.

A Downpour of Division

Estimate the quotients.

1. 87 ÷ 3   2. 2477 ÷ 5   3. 79 ÷ 8   4. 117 ÷ 6   5. 77 ÷ 2

Solve these problems.

6. 5)509   7. 5)$6.50   8. 6)728   9. 40)822   10. 9)91

11. 80)320   12. 7)$0.63   13. 2)837   14. 4)128   15. 5)$7.05

16. On Saturday, Tyesha watched two movies, one right after the other. The first movie was 115 minutes long. The second was 125 minutes long. How many hours did Tyesha watch movies?

17. Carlos has a baseball card album that holds 12 cards on each page. When Carlos counted his cards, he found that he had 504. How many pages will he fill?

If you don't stop, my name will be mud.
Hailing cabs!

Answers from page 62

Tornadoes

Adjectives describe nouns. They tell which one, what kind, how many.

blue hat   **expensive hat**   **fifteen hats**

Adverbs describe verbs, adjectives, or other adverbs. They tell when, where, how, how much, or how often. They often end in the letters **ly**.

ran there   ran then   ran well   ran far   ran frequently

TORNADOES

Called twisters because of their twisting motion, tornadoes are violent, swirling windstorms. Unlike their cousin the hurricane, tornadoes form on land and not over water.

Tornadoes can occur when a swift cold front rushes in under hot, humid air. The warm air rises rapidly and begins to spin.

A black cloud suddenly appears, and a funnel gradually reaches down from it. As the funnel dips down from the sky, it sucks up everything in its path. It whirls things up through its dark funnel, sometimes carrying them for miles before crashing them to the ground. Usually less than an hour long, tornadoes cause tremendous destruction.

There are ten adjectives in this passage about tornadoes. There are two in the first paragraph, five in the second, and three in the third paragraph. Can you find them? List them on the lines below.

First Paragraph	Second Paragraph	Third Paragraph
_____	_____	_____
_____	_____	_____
	_____	_____
	_____	
	_____	

There are four adverbs in this passage. There is one in the second paragraph and there are three in the third paragraph. Write them below.

_____ _____ _____ _____

Circle the correct answer or fill in the blank.

1. The main idea of this passage is _____.

    a. tornadoes bring rain

    b. tornadoes are very powerful storms

    c. tornadoes form on land

2. In the third paragraph, second sentence, to what does the word **it** refer?

    a. tornado

    b. funnel

    c. black cloud

3. Which statement is **not** true?

    a. Tornadoes form on land.

    b. Tornadoes usually last longer than an hour.

    c. Tornadoes cause great damage.

4. Which word in the last sentence means "a very large amount"? _____

5. In the first sentence, what does it mean that a tornado is a cousin of the hurricane?

_____

_____

_____

_____

Find the sum or difference. Simplify the answers.

6. $\dfrac{2}{12} + \dfrac{4}{12} =$

7. $\dfrac{3}{5} + \dfrac{3}{10} =$

8. $\dfrac{9}{12} - \dfrac{1}{3} =$

9. $\dfrac{1}{2} - \dfrac{3}{8} =$

10. $\dfrac{3}{4} + \dfrac{5}{16} =$

11. $\dfrac{8}{9} - \dfrac{2}{9} =$

Flip, Turn, and Slide

Write whether each picture of a congruent figure shows a flip, slide, or a turn.

1.
_____

2.
_____

3.
_____

4.
_____

5.
_____

6.
_____

Tell which figure is congruent and which is similar.

7.

8.

9.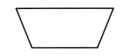

THE FIGHTING GROUND

Read *The Fighting Ground* by Avi. It is the story of a thirteen-year-old boy who cannot wait to go to war to serve his country during the Revolutionary War. After you have read the story, answer the following questions.

1. The chapter headings indicate the time of day. From start to finish, how long does this story last?

   _____

2. Jonathan wants to fight in the Revolutionary War. What is the Revolutionary War, and when did it take place?

   _____

   _____

3. In what state does Jonathan live? (Hint: you are told indirectly on page 5!)

   _____

4. Jonathan is the only character in the entire book given a name. Everyone else is merely given a label such as "his father" or "the Hessian" or "the tavern keeper." What other labels instead of names are used in the book?

   _____

   _____

   Why do you think the author gave only one character a name?

   _____

   _____

5. Why did the Corporal tell the men at first that they would be fighting about 15 enemy soldiers and then later change that number to 20 or 25?

   _____

   _____

   _____

74

6. Did Jonathan have permission from his father to go to war? Explain.

_____

_____

_____

Why do you think Jonathan's father refused to allow Jonathan to go?

_____

_____

_____

7. What language did the Hessians speak? _____
The Hessians were mercenary soldiers, which meant that they fought
for money paid to them by the English. Describe how the Hessians looked
as they advanced toward Jonathan and the other soldiers.

_____

_____

_____

8. At the end of the story, Jonathan enters the house where he had been
held prisoner and he sees that the three Hessians are still asleep. He is
supposed to leave immediately and report to the Corporal that the
Hessians are asleep. The Corporal, along with his soldiers, would then
attack and kill the sleeping Hessians. What does Jonathan do instead? Why?

_____

_____

_____

_____

_____

_____

Often we dream about what something will be like. For example, we can't wait to get to Grandmom's house because we dream of awesome meals and constant entertainment. What we experience when we get there may be quite different. The food might taste a little funny because it's not Mom's. We might get a little bored since Grandmom doesn't have sports equipment or the right videos.

Jonathan dreamed about the glory of fighting for his country. The reality of actually fighting a battle was quite different from what he imagined.

Put yourself in the shoes of Jonathan and write an entry in his journal. The entry should be two paragraphs long, each with a topic sentence and at least two supporting sentences that use facts from the book. In the first paragraph, tell what you thought being a soldier would be like. In the second paragraph, tell what being a soldier was really like.

Dear Journal,

Jonathan

Do you know that Avi has a Web site? Check it out at www.avi-writer.com.

The View from the Cherry Tree

Read *The View from the Cherry Tree* **by Willo Cavis Roberts**

Answer the following questions about what you read.

1. In the beginning of the book, what event do we learn is about to take place that has Rob's household all stirred up?

   _____

2. Where does Rob like to go to get away from his family? _____

3. In the second chapter, from his perch in the tree, Rob overhears his Uncle Ray telling his father something. What did Uncle Ray tell Rob's father?

   _____

4. In Chapter 4, what does Rob do to get back at Mrs. Calloway for hitting him with a broom?

   _____

5. In Chapter 5, what does Rob see from his hiding spot in the cherry tree?

   _____

6. What does Rob see that makes him think it wasn't an accident?

   _____

7. What does Rob's cat do to the man in the house?

   _____

8. In Chapter 6, what happens when Rob tries to tell his father what he saw?

   _____

9. Who is the first person to listen when Rob tells him what he saw? _____

10. Name three things that happen to Rob that make him think that someone is trying to kill him.

   a. _____

   b. _____

   c. _____

11. Circle two reasons Rob's family thinks he's acting strange.

   a. He called the police.

   b. He eats a lot of cherries.

   c. They think he knocked over his cousin.

   d. He doesn't want to help get ready
      for the wedding.

12. At the end of Chapter 11, Rob runs when the police
    come to his house. Why does he run?

   _____

13. Name two people Rob suspects could be the murderer.

   _____   _____

14. How did Rob know for sure who the murderer was?

   _____

15. Why was Mrs. Calloway murdered? Circle the correct answer.

   a. She was really mean.

   b. She had found Derek's drugs and wouldn't give them back.

   c. She wanted Max buy her a new hose.

16. Fiction can be divided into realistic fiction and fantasy. Which type is
    The View from the Cherry Tree ? Tell why.

   _____

   _____

   _____

On My Honor

On My Honor, by Marion Dane Bauer, is a story about the deadly disobedience of two twelve-year-old boys, Tony Zabrinsky and Joel Bates. After you read the book, answer the following questions.

1. At the very beginning of the book, we are told that Tony and Joel are very different people. They are so different that on the second page of the story we are told: "Joel wondered, sometimes, why they stayed friends." Use at least three good sentences to describe how Tony was different from Joel.

   _____

   _____

   _____

   _____

2. What does it mean when we say that someone did something because of peer pressure?

   _____

   _____

3. In the first chapter, why did Joel ask his father if he could bike out to Starved Rock with Tony, even though he did not really want to go?

   _____

   _____

   _____

   _____

4. At the end of the first chapter, Joel says "On my honor." What has he promised to his father?

   _____

   _____

   _____

5. Tony and Joel were planning on climbing the "bluffs." Look up **bluff** in the dictionary and write the meaning that fits the story.

_____

_____

6. What does Tony suggest instead of climbing Starved Rock?

_____

_____

7. What is the Vermillion?

_____

_____

8. Why did Joel challenge Tony to swim out to the sandbar?

_____

_____

9. At the very end of Chapter 7, Joel makes a second promise. What is the promise and to whom does he make the promise?

_____

_____

10. What lie does Joel tell his parents when he returns home from the Vermillion?

_____

_____

11. In Chapter 8, why does Joel's father say, "I feel responsible"?

_____

_____

_____

12. In Chapter 9, Joel starts to remember Tony, thinking that "He and Tony always had so much fun together." This seems very different from the first chapter when Joel wonders why he and Tony were even friends. Why do you think there was this change in attitude?

_____

_____

13. What does Joel keep smelling? _____ Why do you think he smells that?

_____

_____

14. Why does Joel's father punish Joel?

_____

_____

15. After Tony's death, many people feel responsible. Why does Joel feel responsible?

_____

_____

Why does Joel's father feel responsible?

_____

_____

16. What does Joel's father mean when he says in the last few pages, "But we all made choices today, Joel. You, me, Tony. Tony's the only one who doesn't have to live with his choices." What does Joel's father mean?

_____

_____

_____

Poet's Corner

Choose one of the following poetry books or choose one of your own.

Falling Up by Shel Silverstein

The Size of the Sun by Jack Prelutsky

Sports Pages by Arnold Adoff

Talking Wall by Margy Burns Knight

Before you read your book, let's explore some important techniques used by poets.

Poets try to make us see, hear, feel, and sometimes even taste or smell the subject of their poems. In poetry, the words create an image. Poets work very hard at choosing the right words to create a mental picture. They use ordinary words in a special way to create imagery, rhythm, and rhyme.

Read the following poems.

The Four Seasons

Summer
The <u>earth</u> is <u>warm</u>, the <u>sun's ablaze</u>,
it is a time of carefree days;
and bees abuzz that chance to pass
may see me snoozing on the grass.

Fall
The leaves are yellow, red, and brown,
a shower sprinkles softly down;
the air is fragrant, crisp, and cool,
and once again I'm stuck in school.

Winter
The birds are gone, the world is white,
the winds are wild, they chill and bite;
the ground is thick with slush and sleet,
and I can barely feel my feet.

Spring
The fields are rich with daffodils,
a coat of clover cloaks the hills,
and I must dance, and I must sing
to see the beauty of the spring.
Anonymous

A Fly and a Flea in a Flue

A fly and a flea in a flue
Were imprisoned, so what could they do?
    Said the fly, "Let's flee!"
    Said the flea. "Let's fly!"
And they flew though a flaw in the flue.
Anonymous

Imagery: Imagery is creating pictures with words. Poets use images to make us see what they see. The poem "The Four Seasons" creates pictures of the seasons. A list of the images in the poem has been started on the lines below.

Add three more images to the list.

a shower sprinkles softly down

the fields are rich with daffodils

_____

_____

_____

Rhythm: The rhythm of a poem helps to create the emotion that we feel when reading the poem. The rhythm of poetry is much like the beat in music. It is created by syllables, some of which are stressed and some of which are not. Often you have to read a poem aloud to hear the rhythm. In the first line of "The Four Seasons," the underlined words are stressed.

What words are stressed in the first line of "A Fly and a Flea in a Flue"?

_____

_____

Rhyme: Rhyme helps us know what to expect next. A poem has a rhyme scheme when two or more of its lines end with the same sound, or rhyme. "The Four Seasons" uses a simple rhyme scheme for its ending words. Example: **ablaze** and **days**

List three sets of rhyming pairs in the poem.

_____   _____   _____

_____   _____   _____

Alliteration: Another technique used by poets is alliteration, which occurs when two or more words begin with the same letter. The poem "A Fly and a Flea in a Flue" uses this technique in addition to rhyme.

Circle the ten words that begin with the same sound in this poem.

Read some of the poems in the book you chose.
You don't have to read a poetry book in order.

What is the title of the poetry book you chose?

_____

Choose a favorite poem from the ones you read. What is the title?

_____

List three images, or word pictures, that you see in your poem.

_____

_____

_____

Read your poem out loud. Can you hear the rhythm of your poem? Write
the first line of your poem and circle the stressed syllables.

_____

Does your poem have any rhyme? _____ Does it use alliteration? _____

If so, list three sets of rhyming pairs in your poem.

_____   _____   _____

_____   _____   _____

Draw an illustration for your poem.

Summarizing

Have you ever read a great book and then had a hard time trying to summarize the plot for a friend? Often when we summarize we tell too much and don't get to the point.

Summarizing is a surprisingly difficult skill. There are a few rules that may help you do a better job of summarizing. Choose an interesting book to read. Use it to complete these pages.

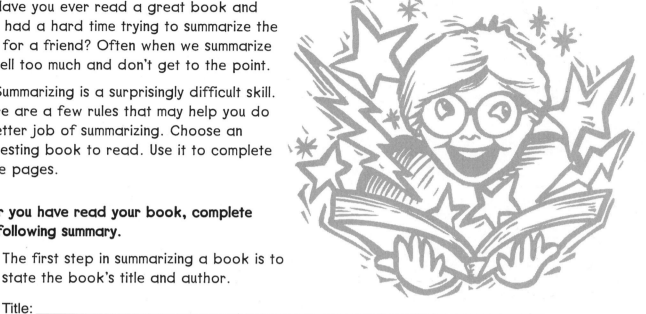

After you have read your book, complete the following summary.

1. The first step in summarizing a book is to state the book's title and author.

    Title: _____

    Author: _____

2. The second step is to write a preliminary sentence telling your reader or listener what the book is mainly about. For example, "This book is a story about a young boy named Michael who must face the divorce of his parents." Or, "This book is about mice called Micelinks who live underground and plot to overthrow humans." Try to summarize your book in one sentence.

    _____

    _____

3. Next, list the three or four major events in your story. Those events should describe the problem or issue in your story. The events should be listed in the order in which they happened. Do not to get too detailed; include only the most important events. Remember, you want the reader or listener to want to read the book and not just your summary.

    1. _____

    _____

2. _____

_____

3. _____

_____

4. _____

_____

4. In one or two sentences, summarize how your story ends.

_____

_____

_____

_____

_____

_____

Draw an important scene from your book.

Wow, That Was Some Story!

Read a book that interests you. Use that book to complete these pages.

Pretend that you are the main character in your book. You must have had quite an adventure! As the main character in your book, what are some of the best things that happened to you?

_____

_____

_____

_____

_____

What are some of the worst things that happened to you?

_____

_____

_____

_____

_____

_____

What was the outcome of your adventure?

_____

_____

_____

_____

_____

Perhaps you would have liked your adventure to have a different outcome. On the following lines, write a new ending for your book.

_____

_____

_____

_____

_____

_____

_____

Write a letter to the author of your book. Tell him or her how you liked your adventure. Describe your favorite parts. Tell the author whether you liked the way the book ended or if you liked your ending better. Explain why.

Dear _____,

_____

_____

_____

_____

_____

_____

_____

_____

_____

_____

_____

_____

Sincerely,

Answer Key

PAGE 2
1. Cro-Magnon Man
2. artifacts
3. Neolithic Period
4. Mesopotamia
5. Pharaoh
6. pyramids
7. Zeus
8. Julius Caesar
9. Middle Ages
10. Charlemagne
11. Muslims
12. Crusades
13. Columbus, de Gama, and Magellan
14. Shakespeare
15. Aztec and Incas
16. Declaration of Independence
17. Louisiana Purchase
18. Industrial Revolution
19. Civil War
20. Orville Wright
21. Henry Ford
22. World Wars
23. Martin Luther King, Jr.
24. Alan Shepard
25. Sandra Day O'Connor
26. Sally Ride

PAGE 7
1-5. map work
6. 20, 140
7. Answers will vary.
8. North America, South America
9. China, Canada

h, f, a ,g, c, d, b, e, i

PAGE 10
1. a. 96,000,506
   b. 74,002,012
   c. 9,402,201
2. a. seven million four hundred twenty-six thousand five
   b. one million twenty
3. a. 500,000
   b. 50,000
   c. 50
4. a. 7,000
   b. 739,400
   c. 100,000
5. a. $20.28
   b. $25.11
6. a. 1 dime, 3 nickels
   b. 1 nickel, 5 pennies
   c. 3 dimes, 2 nickels
7. a. 2 pennies, 2 one-dollar bills
   b. 2 pennies, 1 dime, 4 one-dollar bills
8. a. 652,640   719,820   752,800
   b. 320,300   324,400   346,879
9. a. 5 hours 50 minutes
   b. 22 hours 30 minutes

10. a. 850
    b. 450
    c. 570
    d. 600
11. a. $26.29
    b. 4009
    c. 4518
12. 462

PAGE 13
1. Handle/moisture; handled; handled/refrigerated; handled/not toasted; handled/toasted
2. Handled, mold spores from hand get on bread
3. Not toasted, toasting helps sterilize the bread
4. Room temperature, mold does not grow as well in cold
5. Moisture, mold grows well in moisture
6. Wash hands before handling food, handle food as little as possible, refrigerate food, sterilize food by cooking

PAGE 14
1. cannot
2. RSVP
3. Thomas Jefferson
4. Australia
5. once
6. Mt. Everest
7. Pacific Ocean
8. Colorado
9. cathedral
10. USA
11. 24 hours
12. Europe
13. cousin
14. George Washington
15. Egypt
16. cold-blooded
17. southern
18. Asia
19. IX
20. 6 inches
21. lord
22. Washington, D.C.
23. desert
24. The Crusades
25. Eastern Hemisphere
26. water
27. leap year
28. Betsy Ross

1. peas
2. hand
3. quarterback
4. figure skating
5. Detroit
6. lizard

PAGE 16
1. 8 buses
2. 34 rock samples
3. 4 pages
4. 8,708 feet
5. 10 boxes

PAGE 18
1. c
2. b
3. a
4. loyalty
5. a
6. fact, opinion

PAGE 19
1. famous
2. play
3. street
4. dry
5. south
6. coastal
7. computer
8. the National League

PAGE 20

1.	6924 +2173	26 min 48 s −3 min 22 s	10 ft 8 in −9 ft 6 in
	9097	23 min 26 s	1 ft 2 in

2. a. $\frac{9}{100}$

   b. $\frac{9}{10}$

   c. 9

3. a. 6.7, 6.70

   b. 10.40, 10.4

4. a. eight hundred sixty-nine and fifty-three hundredths

   b. nine and eight hundred seventy-one thousandths

5. a. 12.003

   b. 600,042.73

6. $111.65

7. 4725 yards

8. 8.52   314.6   13.64

9. a. 9:50

   b. 4:00

10. 20 word problems

11. a. 5652

    b. 35,581

12. a. 74 R6

    b. 98 R3

13. a. 4 1/4

    b. 4

    c. 2700

14. 6 and 7

15. 100   10,000

16. Redskins

PAGE 22

1. The immigrant's trip to America was stressful.
2. a. This was their first trip away from home.
   b. The immigrants left behind family.
   c. The conditions on the boat were difficult.
   d. America was an unfamiliar land.
4. Many immigrants have said the trip was well worth it.

PAGE 24

5. about 7 times
6. Number of People to Reach the Top of Mt. Everest
7. Year; Number of People
10. 1993

PAGE 26

1. Philadelphia, Pennsylvania
2. Washington, D. C.
3. Minneapolis, St. Paul
4. Arizona, New Mexico, Utah, Colorado
5. Washington, Oregon, California
6. Antarctica
7. China
8. Nepal and Tibet
9. Kenya, Uganda, Tanzania

PAGE 28

1. b
2. c
3. a
4. c
5. c
6. a. archaeologists
   b. competitors
7. a. skirmishes
   b. truce
   c. spectators
8. a. traditions
   b. pagan
   c. corrupt

9. b
10. a

PAGE 31

Both were all-girl teams!

PAGE 32

1. f   6. e
2. d   7. j
3. h   8. c
4. a   9. g
5. b   10. i

16. rectangle or parallelogram
17. square or rhombus
18. parallelogram
19. rhombus or parallelogram
20. trapezoid

23. rectangle
24. AC, BD or AB, CD

31. point

PAGE 35

1. b
2. Answers will vary.
3. c
4. torch, flag, hymn, oath
5. boycotted

PAGE 37

1. $1\frac{1}{8}$

2. 2

3. $2\frac{2}{4}$ or $2\frac{1}{2}$

4. $7\frac{2}{3}$

5. $4\frac{1}{2}$

6. 5

7. $\frac{17}{6}$

8. $\frac{22}{5}$

9. $\frac{24}{7}$

10. $\frac{25}{2}$

11. $\frac{45}{6}$

12. $\frac{28}{3}$

13. $\frac{8}{2}$

14. $\frac{27}{3}$

15. 11 times

PAGE 40

1. b
2. T   T   F
3. b
4. object
5. a

1. 2814   2. 35,670   3. 1386   4. 1154   5. 1860
6. 78,364   7. 192   8. $61.32   9. 1411   10. $367.29

PAGE 42

1. sphere   2. cube   3. rectangular prism   4. pyramid
5. cone   6. cylinder 7. square
8. circle
9. rectangle

10. cube
11. sphere
12. cylinder
13. pyramid
14. 1 foot 6 inches
15. 6 yards 1 foot

PAGE 43

1-6. Answers will vary.

7. $\frac{2}{3}$

8. $\frac{2}{5}$

9. $\frac{4}{5}$

10. $\frac{1}{8}$

11. $\frac{3}{4}$

12. $\frac{1}{2}$

13. $\frac{1}{3}$

14. $\frac{7}{10}$

15. $\frac{1}{4}$

PAGE 44

1. the balloon
2. the tighter drumhead
3. the tighter drumhead
4. The snare drum has a higher sound. It must vibrate faster than a kettle drum.

PAGE 45

1. a.
2. b.

PAGE 46

1. 15.3	5. 18.7
2. 9.54	6. 28.5
3. 19.58	7. 6.0
4. 81.77	8. 28,000

PAGE 48

1. e	3. c
2. b	4. wind

PAGE 50

1. b
2. a, d
3. a
4. warm front and cold front

PAGE 51

1. 10
2. 6
3. 10
4. 16
5. 6
6. 12
7. $5\frac{1}{3}$
8. $\frac{1}{3}$ of the animals, or 6

PAGE 52

told, did, whistled, tossed, shook, whirled, sent, swept, blew, woke

1. Answers will vary.
2. "And wake the flowers from sleep"
3. the March Wind
4. Answers will vary.

5. branches, day
6. frozen, live-long
7. round, up, down
8. you, I
9. and
10. upon, from
11. Woo–oo!

PAGE 56

1. 13 hours 1 minute
2. 9 hours 11 minutes
3. 9:30 PM
4. thirty and five hundredths
5. 3.09 or 3.10
6. 30.00 30.05 30.06 30.08 30.11
   76 82 85 86 96
7. 30.06
8. 85
9. 11
10. 20
11. 30.06
12. 85
13. 5 0 2 8 9
14. 20,158,983,000
    20,158,000,000
    20,000,000,000

PAGE 59

1. noon
2. cold front, warm front
3. east   south
4. Philadelphia   Denver   Denver
5. a
6. c
7. d
8. cold and rainy
9. warm

PAGE 61

1. 28 inches
2. 27 inches
3. 30 inches
4. 18 inches, 14 square inches
5. 18 inches, 18 square inches
6. 20 inches, 24 square inches
7. 36 inches, 81 square inches
8. 1 foot
9. 36 feet, 80 square feet
10. 24 cubic inches
11. 48 cubic inches
12. 36 cubic inches
13. 60 cubic inches
14. 6160 cubic feet
15. 3 inches, 48 cubic inches

PAGE 63

2. Hurricanes start out as tropical storms, but they become hurricanes when their winds reach 75 miles per hour.
3. In other parts of the world, hurricanes are called typhoons, cyclones, and willy-willies.
4. Hurricanes occur most often in the states of Texas, Florida, and Louisiana.
5. Over 6,000 people were killed when a hurricane struck Galveston, Texas, on August 27, 1900.
6. The U.S. National Weather Service, an agency of the federal government, started naming hurricanes in 1953.
7. Hurricanes are given people's names in the order of the

alphabet: Abby, Bob, Cathy, Danny, Elizabeth, Frank, and so on.

8. "Mom, have you ever heard of a hurricane named Zelda?" asked Becky.
9. "Goodness me! I never have, " replied her mother.
10. They alternate male and female.
11. Very few names start with those letters.

PAGE 64

1. <	11. 28
2. >	12. 300
3. >	13. 29
4. =	14. $\frac{12}{18}$
5. <	15. 51
6. >	16. 7
7. 6	17. 600
8. 12	18. 15
9. 1	19. 7
10. 18	20. 9

PAGE 66

Answers will vary. The barometer works because the air pressure pushes down on the balloon. When the air pressures rises, there is more pressure on the balloon and the straw moves up.

PAGE 69

1. 30	10. 10 R1
2. 500	11. 40
3. 10	12. $ .09
4. 20	13. 418 R1
5. 40	14. 32
6. 101 R4	15. $1.41
7. $1.30	16. 4 hours
8. 121 R2	17. 42 pages
9. 20 R22	

PAGES 70

violent	swift	black
swirl	cold	dark
	hot	tremendous
	humid	
	warm	

rapidly	suddenly	gradually	usually

1. b
2. b
3. b
4. tremendous
5. They are a lot alike.
6. $\frac{1}{2}$
7. $\frac{9}{10}$
8. $\frac{5}{12}$
9. $\frac{1}{8}$
10. $1\frac{1}{16}$
11. $\frac{2}{3}$

PAGE 72

1. flip	6. flip
2. slide	7. similar, congruent
3. flip	8. similar, congruent
4. turn	9. congruent, similar
5. slide	

PAGE 74

1. 1 day and 32 minutes
2. Around 1776 the colonies fought to free themselves from Britain.
3. New Jersey
4. Answers will vary.
5. so the men would not panic
6. No. He misled his mother.
   Jonathan's father had seen war and knew how horrible it was.
7. German
   The Hessians looked organized and big.
8. Jonathan feels sorry that the soldiers will be killed. He wakes them up with the intention that they surrender.

PAGE 77

1. Rob's sister is getting married.
2. the cherry tree in his yard
3. that he took money from his employer
4. He puts ketchup on himself and pretends that he is hurt.
5. He sees Mrs. Calloway fall from a window.
6. He sees the hands of a man who pushed her.
7. He jumps on him and scratches his arms.
8. Rob's father is too busy to listen to him.
9. Derek
10. He gets shot at.
    A flower pot drops and nearly hits him.
    His food is poisoned.
11. a, c
12. He thought they were going to arrest him.
13. Max and Derek
14. He saw the scratches on his arms.
15. b
16. realistic fiction

PAGE 79

1. Answers will vary. Essentially, Joel does not like to take chances and Tony is a daredevil.
2. doing something because friends of the same age expect it
3. Tony wanted his dad to say no, so that Tony would not have to say it and look bad.
4. He has promised to be careful and not go anywhere except the park.
5. bluff: a steep bank
6. swimming in the river
7. the name of the river
8. because he thought it would be safer than climbing the bluffs
9. He promises the boy who helped that he would go to the police and report Tony missing.
10. Joel says that he was too tired and that Tony had gone all the way to Starved Rock by himself.
11. Joel's father feels responsible for so easily giving permission to Tony and Joel to take the bike ride in the first place.
12. Answers will vary. Often, however, when people die, we think about them in a different light.
13. the river
    Answers will vary.
14. Tony's death had punished Joel more than enough.
15. Joel's father and Joel made some poor choices and were alive to be guilty about them. Tony also was responsible for making poor choices, but he was dead and doesn't have to live with the guilt.